MENSA
WORD
PUZZLES

THIS IS A CARLTON BOOK

Text & puzzle copyright © British Mensa Limited 1993
Design and artwork copyright © Carlton Books
Limited 1999

This Edition published by Carlton Books Limited 1999

A CIP catalogue for this book is available from the
British Library

ISBN 1 85868 308 4

Printed and bound in Great Britain

MENSA
WORD
PUZZLES

Harold Gale

CARLTON

AMERICAN MENSA

American Mensa Ltd is an organization for people who have one common trait: an IQ in the top 2% of the nation. Over 50,000 current members have found out how smart they are. This leaves room for an additional 4.5 million members in America alone. You may be one of them.

If you enjoy mental exercise, you'll find lots of good "workout programs" in the *Mensa Bulletin,* our national magazine. Voice your opinion in one of the newsletters published by each of our 150 local chapters. Learn from the many books and publications that are available to you as a member.

Are you a "people person," or would you like to meet other people with whom you feel comfortable? Then come to our local meetings, parties, and get-togethers. Participate in our lectures and debates. Attend our regional events and national gatherings. There's something happening on the Mensa calendar almost daily. So, you have lots of opportunities to meet people, exchange ideas, and make interesting new friends. Maybe you're looking for others who share your special interest? Whether yours is as common as crossword puzzles or as esoteric as Egyptology, there's a Mensa Special Interest Group (SIG) for it.

Take the challenge. Find out how smart you really are. Contact American Mensa Ltd today and ask for a free brochure. We enjoy adding new members and ideas to our high-IQ organization.

American Mensa Ltd,
1229 Corporate Drive West,
Arlington, TX 76006-6103.

Or, if you don't live in the USA and you'd like more details, you can contact Mensa International, 15 The Ivories, 628 Northampton Street, London N1 2NY, England, who will be happy to put you in touch with your own national Mensa.

INTRODUCTION

Puzzles which involved the use of the English language are notoriously difficult to produce. Unfortunately the differences between the different variants of the language are often profound. This book uses words which, hopefully, are truly international, and can be found in Webster's New World Dictionary as well as the Collins English Dictionary. Word puzzles are great fun though, and are more than worth the effort involved in their production.

Harold Gale always insisted that credit should go to his extremely able helpers in putting this book together. Carolyn Skitt checked, criticized and improved on many of the puzzles produced. Without her help, this book might still have been in the making. Help also came from other quarters. Bobby Raikhy worked on the many diagrammatic styles you'll find within these pages, and puzzler David Ballheimer checked the proofs and made sure that everything worked.

All in all, I know you'll be pleased with the results.

Robert Allen,
Editorial Director,
Mensa Publications.

WORD PUZZLE 1

Place one letter in the middle of this diagram. Four five-letter words can now be rearranged from each straight line of letters. What is the letter and what are the words?

ANSWER 62

WORD PUZZLE 2

Arrange the tiles in this diagram so that they form a square. When this is done correctly four words can be read down and across. What are the words?

ANSWER 10

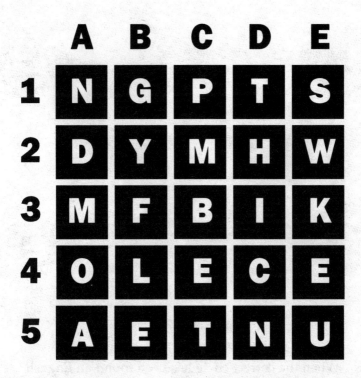

	A	B	C	D	E
1	N	G	P	T	S
2	D	Y	M	H	W
3	M	F	B	I	K
4	O	L	E	C	E
5	A	E	T	N	U

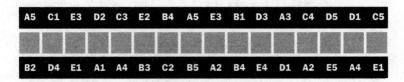

A5	C1	E3	D2	C3	E2	B4	A5	E3	B1	D3	A3	C4	D5	D1	C5
B2	D4	E1	A1	A4	B3	C2	B5	A2	B4	E4	D1	A2	E5	A4	E1

WORD PUZZLE 3

Select one of the two letters from the grid, in accordance with the reference shown, and place it in the word frame. When the correct letters have been chosen a sixteen-letter word can be read. What is the word?

ANSWER 103

WORD PUZZLE 4

Make a circle out of these shapes.
When the correct circle has been found an English
word can be read clockwise. What is the word?

ANSWER 51

WORD PUZZLE 5

Move from circle to touching circle collecting the
letters of GOLD. Always start at the G.
How many different ways are there to do this?

ANSWER 92

BEAST	ADDER
DECOR	PILAF
HERON	PYGMY
BATON	TAXIS
HUMAN	ROUND

WORD PUZZLE 6

Six of the words in the diagram are associated for some reason. Find the words and then work out whether SHELL belongs to the group.

ANSWER 40

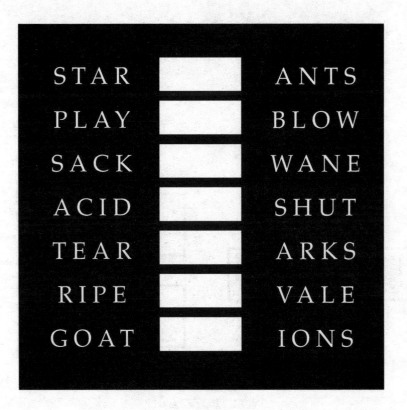

STAR   ANTS

PLAY   BLOW

SACK   WANE

ACID   SHUT

TEAR   ARKS

RIPE   VALE

GOAT   IONS

WORD PUZZLE 7

Change the second letter of each word to the left
and the right. Two other English words must be
formed. Place the letter used in the empty section.
When this has been completed for all the words
another English word can be read down.
What is the word?

ANSWER 82

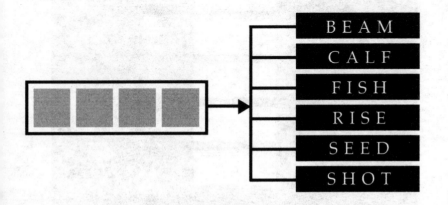

WORD PUZZLE 8

Which English word of four letters can be attached
to the front of the words shown in the diagram to
create six other words?

ANSWER 30

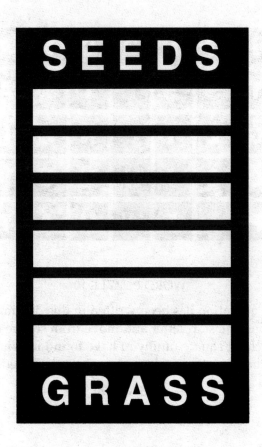

WORD PUZZLE 9

Complete the word ladder by changing one letter of each word per step. The newly created word must be found in the dictionary. What are the words to turn SEEDS to GRASS?

ANSWER 72

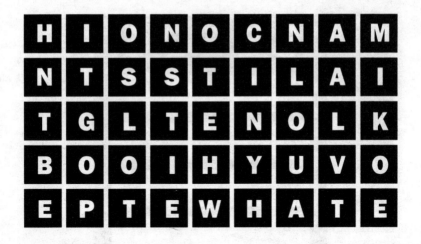

H	I	O	N	O	C	N	A	M
N	T	S	S	T	I	L	A	I
T	G	L	T	E	N	O	L	K
B	O	O	I	H	Y	U	V	O
E	P	T	E	W	H	A	T	E

WORD PUZZLE 10

A quotation has been written in this diagram.
Find the start letter and move from square to
touching square until you have found it. What is
the quotation and to whom is it attributed?

ANSWER 20

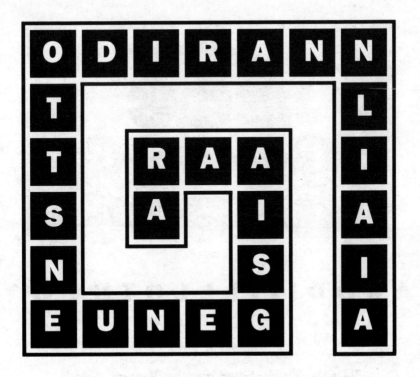

WORD PUZZLE 11

The names of three countries are to be found in the
diagram. The letters of the names are in the order
they normally appear. What are the countries?

ANSWER 61

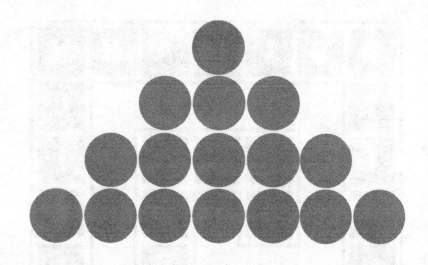

A A D D I I I L L L Q T U V W Y

WORD PUZZLE 12

Place the letters shown into the diagram in such a way that three words can be read across and one down the middle.
What are the words?

ANSWER 9

WORD PUZZLE 13

Start at the bottom letter M and move from circle to touching circle to the N at the top right. How many different ways are there of collecting the nine letters of MANHATTAN?

ANSWER 102

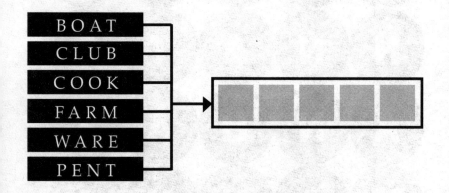

WORD PUZZLE 14

Which English word of five letters can be attached
to the back of the words shown in the diagram to
create six other words?

ANSWER 50

WORD PUZZLE 15

Select one letter from each of the segments.
When the correct letters have been found a word of
eight letters can be read clockwise.
What is the word?

ANSWER 91

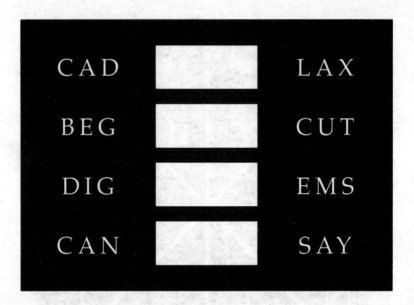

WORD PUZZLE 16

Place two letters in the empty space which, when added to the end of the words to the left and to the beginning of the right, form other English words. When this is completed another word can be read downwards. What is the word?

ANSWER 39

N	O	F	S
Q	O	E	E
C	A	R	Y
M	U	T	S

WORD PUZZLE 17

Take the letters and arrange them correctly in the
column under which they appear. Once this has
been done an historical character will appear.
Who is the person?

ANSWER 81

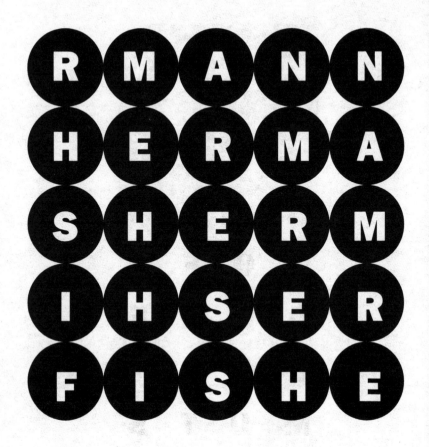

WORD PUZZLE 18

Start at the bottom letter F and move from circle to
touching circle to the N at the top right. How many
different ways are there of collecting the nine
letters of FISHERMAN?

ANSWER 29

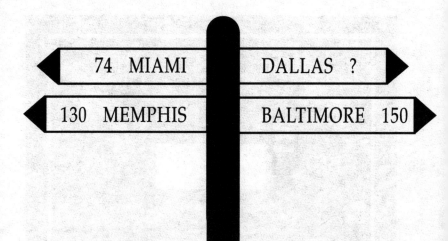

WORD PUZZLE 19

This is a meaningless signpost but there is a
twisted form of logic behind the figures. Discover
the logic and find the distance to Dallas.
How far is it?

ANSWER 71

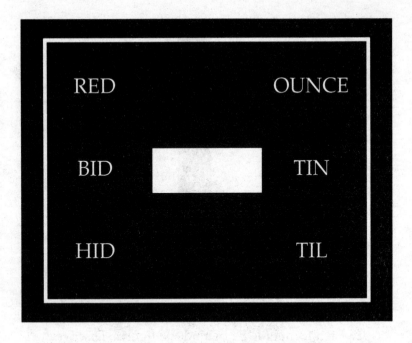

RED   OUNCE

BID   TIN

HID   TIL

WORD PUZZLE 20

Place an English word of THREE letters in the empty space. This word, when added to the end of the three words to the left and to the beginning of the three words to the right, will form six other words. What is the word?

ANSWER 19

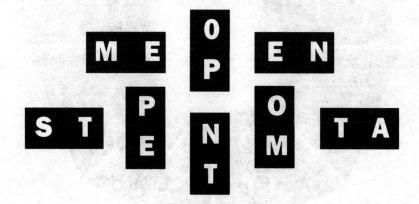

WORD PUZZLE 21

Arrange the tiles in this diagram so that they form
a square. When this is done correctly four words
can be read down and across. What are the words?

ANSWER 8

WORD PUZZLE 22

Place one letter in the middle of this diagram. Four five-letter words can now be rearranged from each straight line of letters. What is the letter and what are the words?

ANSWER 60

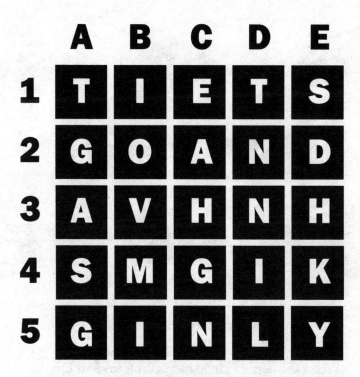

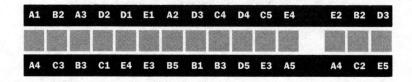

WORD PUZZLE 23

Select one of the two letters from the grid, in accordance with the reference shown, and place it in the word frame. When the correct letters have been chosen an occasion can be read.
What is the occasion?

ANSWER 101

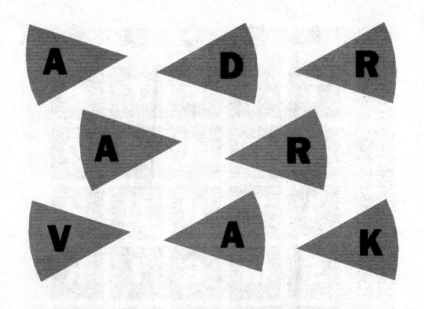

WORD PUZZLE 24

Make a circle out of these shapes.
When the correct circle has been found an English
word can be read clockwise. What is the word?

ANSWER 49

BURNT	EVENT
COUNT	CADET
MERIT	FAULT
FLINT	CARAT
ABBOT	GIANT

WORD PUZZLE 25

Five of the words in the diagram are associated for some reason. Find the words and then work out whether PLANT belongs to the group.

ANSWER 90

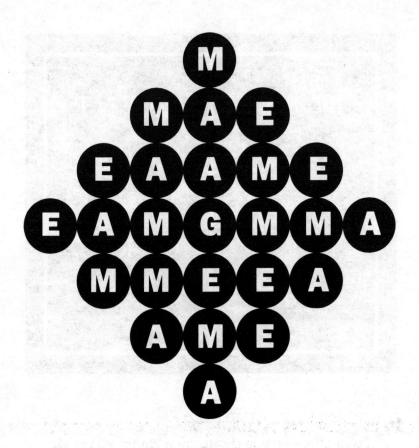

WORD PUZZLE 26

Move from circle to touching circle collecting the
letters of GAME. Always start at the G.
How many different ways are there to do this?

ANSWER 38

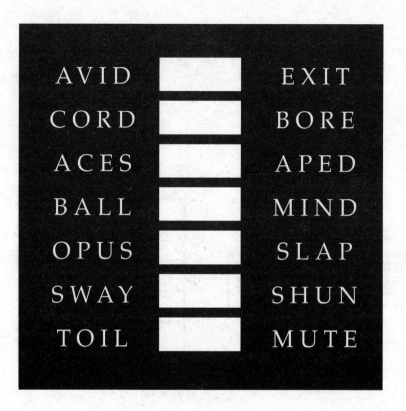

AVID		EXIT
CORD		BORE
ACES		APED
BALL		MIND
OPUS		SLAP
SWAY		SHUN
TOIL		MUTE

WORD PUZZLE 27

Change the second letter of each word to the left and the right. Two other English words must be formed. Place the letter used in the empty section. When this has been completed for all the words another English word can be read down. What is the word?

ANSWER 80

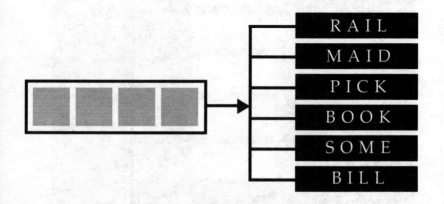

WORD PUZZLE 28

Which English word of four letters can be attached
to the front of the words shown in the diagram to
create six other words?

ANSWER 28

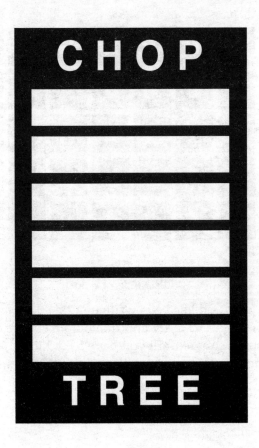

WORD PUZZLE 29

Complete the word ladder by changing one letter
of each word per step. The newly created word
must be found in the dictionary. What are the
words to turn CHOP to TREE?

ANSWER 70

E	H	O	P	E	K	T	T
N	T	C	U	E	A	H	D
I	K	T	I	E	H	E	N
E	O	F	Y	U	A	T	A
H	T	F	O	C	N	T	S

WORD PUZZLE 30

A quotation has been written in this diagram. Find the start letter and move from square to touching square until you have found it. What is the quotation and to whom is it attributed?

ANSWER 18

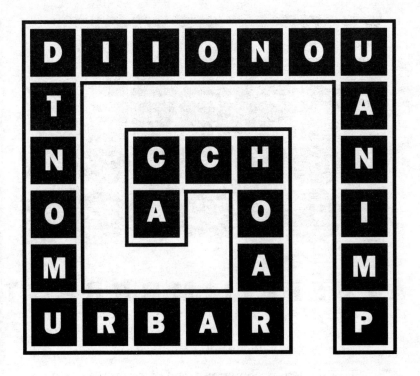

WORD PUZZLE 31

The names of four musical instruments are to be
found in the diagram. The letters of the names are
in the order they normally appear. What are the
musical instruments?

ANSWER 59

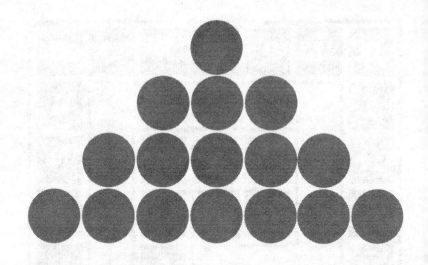

AEFFFFIIIMRRRRST

WORD PUZZLE 32

Place the letters shown into the diagram in such a
way that three words can be read across and one
down the middle.
What are the words?

ANSWER 7

WORD PUZZLE 33

Start at the bottom letter N and move from circle to touching circle to the E at the top right. How many different ways are there of collecting the nine letters of NECTARINE?

ANSWER 100

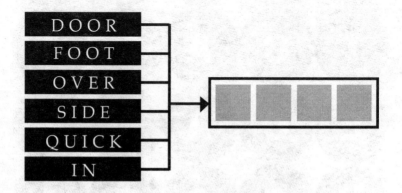

WORD PUZZLE 34

Which English word of four letters can be attached
to the back of the words shown in the diagram to
create six other words?

ANSWER 48

WORD PUZZLE 35

Select one letter from each of the segments.
When the correct letters have been found a word of
eight letters can be read clockwise.
What is the word?

ANSWER 89

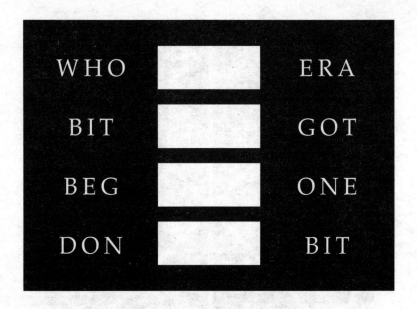

WHO		ERA
BIT		GOT
BEG		ONE
DON		BIT

WORD PUZZLE 36

Place two letters in the empty space which, when added to the end of the words to the left and to the beginning of the right, form other English words. When this is completed another word can be read down. What is the word?

ANSWER 37

R R E N

T S A S

O E I M

M H C A

WORD PUZZLE 37

Take the letters and arrange them correctly in the
column under which they appear. Once this has
been done a famous person will appear.
Who is the person?

ANSWER 79

AFTER THE DOUBLE WEDDING, THE TWO • • • • • • WALKED THROUGH THE HALL, WHICH WAS LITTERED WITH THE • • • • • • FROM THE PARTY HELD THE PREVIOUS NIGHT.

WORD PUZZLE 38

Two words using the same letters in their construction can be used to replace the dots in this sentence. The sentence will then make sense. Each dot is one letter. What are the words?

ANSWER 27

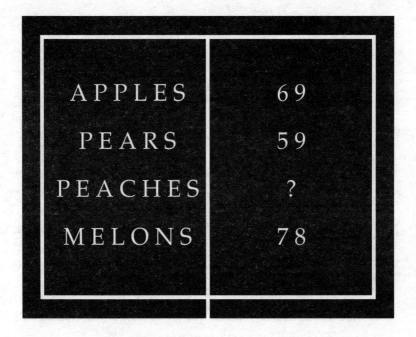

APPLES	69
PEARS	59
PEACHES	?
MELONS	78

WORD PUZZLE 39

Here are some fruit. The number of each is set
alongside the name of the fruit in the diagram.
There is a relationship between the number
and the letters of the names.
How many peaches are there?

ANSWER 69

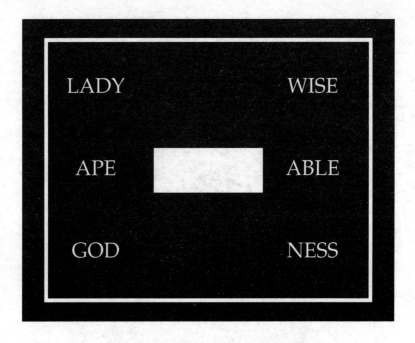

LADY   WISE

APE   ABLE

GOD   NESS

WORD PUZZLE 40

Place an English word of FOUR letters in the
empty space. This word, when added to the end of
the three words to the left and to the beginning of
the three words to the right, will form six other
words. What is the word?

ANSWER 17

WORD PUZZLE 41

Place one letter in the middle of this diagram. Four five-letter words can now be rearranged from each straight line of letters. What is the letter and what are the words?

ANSWER 58

WORD PUZZLE 42

Arrange the tiles in this diagram so that they form
a square. When this is done correctly four words
can be read downwards and across.
What are the words?

ANSWER 6

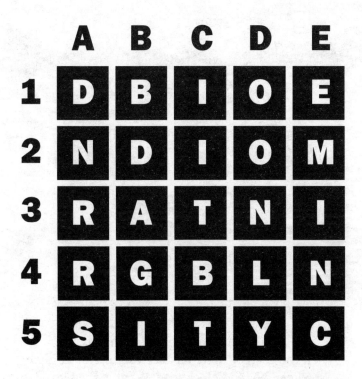

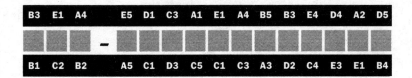

WORD PUZZLE 43

Select one of the two letters from the grid, in accordance with the reference shown, and place it in the word frame. When the correct letters have been chosen a (hyphenated) word can be read. What is the word?

ANSWER 99

WORD PUZZLE 44

Make a circle out of these shapes.
When the correct circle has been found an English
word can be read clockwise. What is the word?

ANSWER 47

CARGO	CEDAR
SEDAN	AGAVE
HEDGE	EMBER
DIGIT	MEDAL
PILOT	WEDGE

WORD PUZZLE 45

Five of the words in the diagram are associated for some reason. Find the words and then work out whether SYRUP belongs to the group.

ANSWER 88

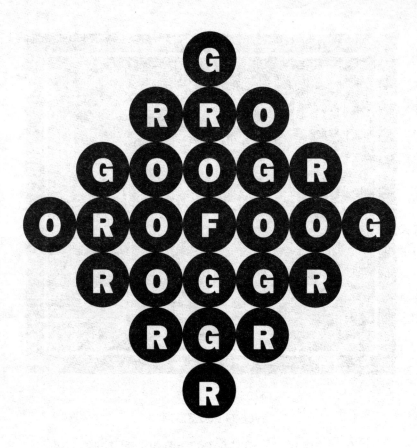

WORD PUZZLE 46

Move from circle to touching circle collecting the
letters of FROG. Always start at the F.
How many different ways are there to do this?

ANSWER 36

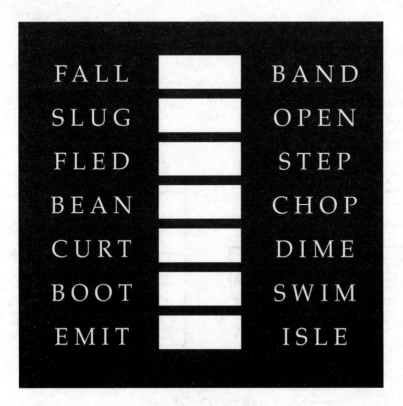

FALL		BAND
SLUG		OPEN
FLED		STEP
BEAN		CHOP
CURT		DIME
BOOT		SWIM
EMIT		ISLE

WORD PUZZLE 47

Change the second letter of each word to the left
and the right. Two other English words must be
formed. Place the letter used in the empty section.
When this has been completed for all the words
another English word can be read down.
What is the word?

ANSWER 78

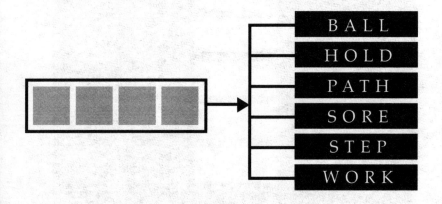

BALL
HOLD
PATH
SORE
STEP
WORK

WORD PUZZLE 48

Which English word of four letters can be attached
to the front of the words shown in the diagram to
create six other words?

ANSWER 26

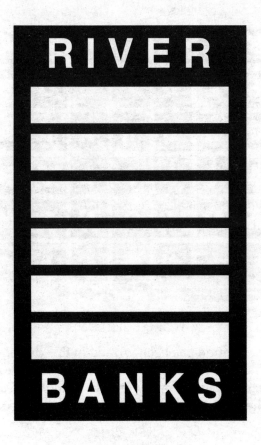

WORD PUZZLE 49

Complete the word ladder by changing one letter of each word per step. The newly created word must be found in the dictionary. What are the words to turn RIVER to BANKS?

ANSWER 68

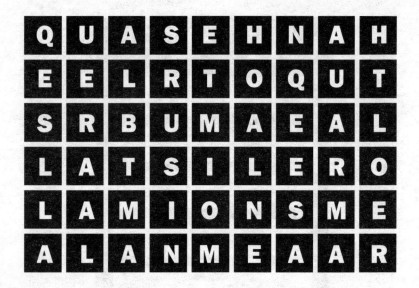

WORD PUZZLE 50

A quotation has been written in this diagram.
Find the start letter and move from square to
touching square until you have found it. What is
the quotation and to whom is it attributed?

ANSWER 16

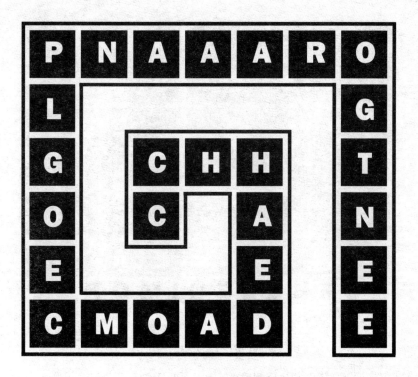

WORD PUZZLE 51

The names of three drinks are to be found in the diagram. The letters of the names are in the order they normally appear. What are the drinks?

ANSWER 57

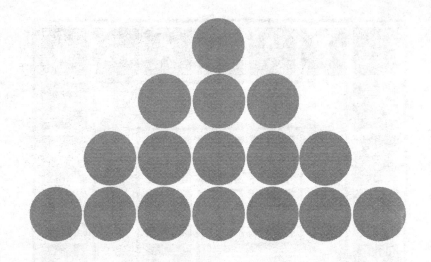

A B C E E E E E G I M O R S V Y

WORD PUZZLE 52

Place the letters shown into the diagram in such a
way that three words can be read across and one
down the middle. What are the words?

ANSWER 5

WORD PUZZLE 53

Start at the letter L and move from circle to
touching circle to the H at the top right. How many
different ways are there of collecting the nine
letters of LABYRINTH?

ANSWER 98

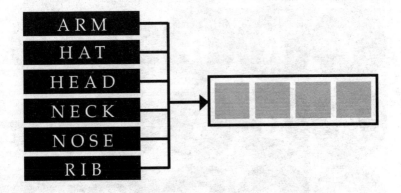

ARM
HAT
HEAD
NECK
NOSE
RIB

WORD PUZZLE 54

Which English word of four letters can be attached
to the back of the words shown in the diagram to
create six other words?

ANSWER 46

WORD PUZZLE 55

Select one letter from each of the segments.
When the correct letters have been found a word of
eight letters can be read clockwise.
What is the word?

ANSWER 87

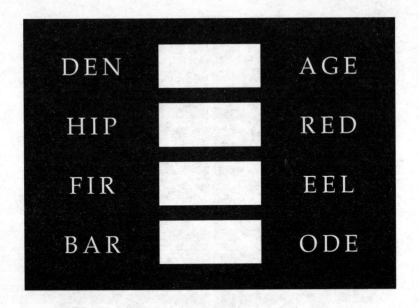

WORD PUZZLE 56

Place two letters in the empty space which, when
added to the end of the words to the left and to the
beginning of the right, form other English words.
When this is completed another word
can be read downwards. What is the word?

ANSWER 35

P H M V

O Y O E

T L W S

E D E H

WORD PUZZLE 57

Take the letters and arrange them correctly in the
column under which they appear.
Once this has been done a movie title will appear.
What is the movie?

ANSWER 77

AUSTRALIA	960
MADAGASCAR	1152
IRELAND	576
CUBA	?

WORD PUZZLE 58

The distances on this departure board are fictitious.
They bear a relationship to the letters in the names,
What should replace the question mark ?

ANSWER 25

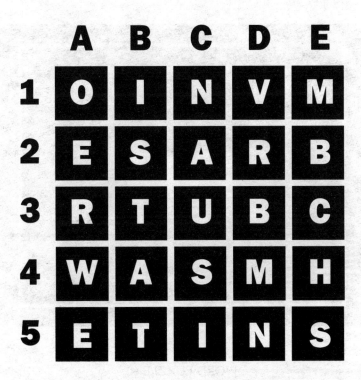

	A	B	C	D	E
1	O	I	N	V	M
2	E	S	A	R	B
3	R	T	U	B	C
4	W	A	S	M	H
5	E	T	I	N	S

B2	B1	D4	D5	A2	A3		B2	C2	D3	B4	B5	B3	A1	E5	C4

A4	C3	C1	E1	A5	D4		D1	C2	E3	E2	C2	C5	E4	D5	A1

WORD PUZZLE 59

Select one of the two letters from the grid, in accordance with the reference shown, and place it in the word frame. When the correct letters have been chosen two linked words can be read. What are the words?

ANSWER 67

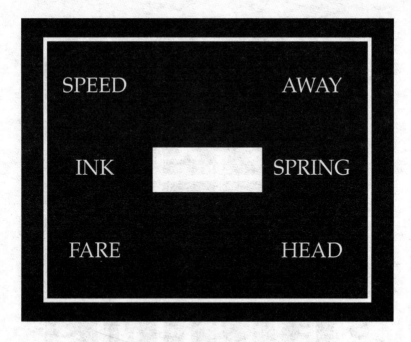

SPEED

AWAY

INK

SPRING

FARE

HEAD

WORD PUZZLE 60

Place an English word of FOUR letters in the empty space. This word, when added to the end of the three words to the left and to the beginning of the three words to the right, will form six other words. What is the word?

ANSWER 15

WORD PUZZLE 61

Place one letter in the middle of this diagram.
Four five-letter words can now be rearranged from
each straight line of letters. What is the letter and
what are the words?

ANSWER 56

WORD PUZZLE 62

Arrange the tiles in this diagram so that they form
a square. When this is done correctly four words
can be read down and across. What are the words?

ANSWER 4

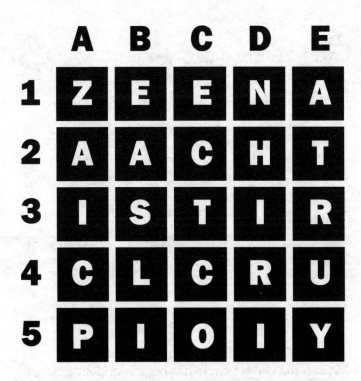

	A	B	C	D	E
1	Z	E	E	N	A
2	A	A	C	H	T
3	I	S	T	I	R
4	C	L	C	R	U
5	P	I	O	I	Y

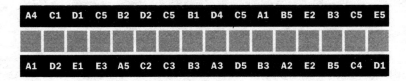

A4	C1	D1	C5	B2	D2	C5	B1	D4	C5	A1	B5	E2	B3	C5	E5
A1	D2	E1	E3	A5	C2	C3	B3	A3	D5	B3	A2	E2	B5	C4	D1

WORD PUZZLE 63

Select one of the two letters from the grid, in accordance with the reference shown, and place it in the word frame. When the correct letters have been chosen a sixteen-letter word can be read. What is the word?

ANSWER 97

WORD PUZZLE 64

Make a circle out of these shapes.
When the correct circle has been found an English
word can be read clockwise. What is the word?

ANSWER 45

COYPU	MAYOR
AROMA	BISON
NYMPH	NIGHT
IDYLL	RABBI
BUYER	ABYSS

WORD PUZZLE 65

Five of the words in the diagram are associated for some reason. Find the words and then work out whether STYLE belongs to the group.

ANSWER 86

WORD PUZZLE 66

Move from circle to touching circle collecting the
letters of BELL. Always start at the B.
How many different ways are there to do this?

ANSWER 34

WORD PUZZLE 67

Change the second letter of each word to the left
and the right. Two other English words must be
formed. Place the letter used in the empty section.
When this has been completed for all the words
another English word can be read down.
What is the word?

ANSWER 76

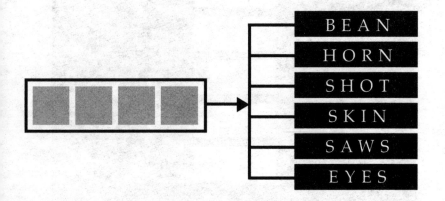

BEAN
HORN
SHOT
SKIN
SAWS
EYES

WORD PUZZLE 68

Which English word of four letters can be attached
to the front of the words shown in the diagram to
create six other words?

ANSWER 24

WORD PUZZLE 69

Complete the word ladder by changing one letter
of each word per step. The newly created word
must be found in the dictionary. What are the
words to turn PONY to CART?

ANSWER 66

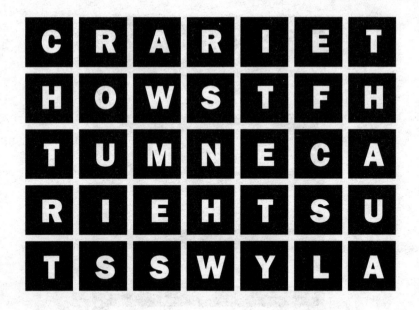

C	R	A	R	I	E	T
H	O	W	S	T	F	H
T	U	M	N	E	C	A
R	I	E	H	T	S	U
T	S	S	W	Y	L	A

WORD PUZZLE 70

A quotation has been written in this diagram.
Find the start letter and move from square to
touching square until you have found it. What is
the quotation and to whom is it attributed?

ANSWER 14

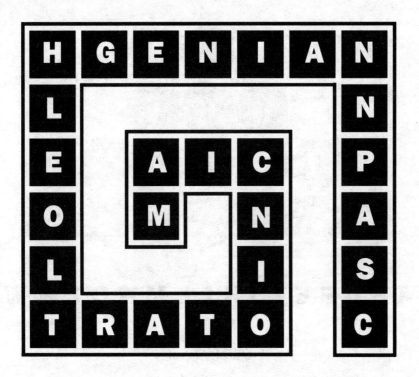

WORD PUZZLE 71

The names of three foods are to be found in the
diagram. The letters of the names are in the order
they normally appear. What are the foods?

ANSWER 55

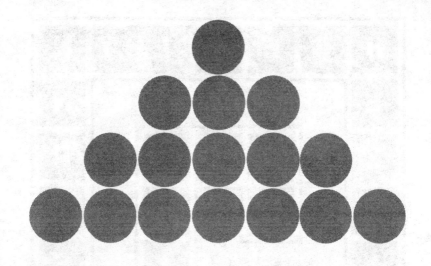

A B D E E E J K L L M N O T W W

WORD PUZZLE 72

Place the letters shown into the diagram in such a way that three words can be read across and one down the middle. What are the words?

ANSWER 3

WORD PUZZLE 73

Start at the letter B and move from circle to
touching circle to the A at the top right. How many
different ways are there of collecting the nine
letters of BALLERINA?

ANSWER 96

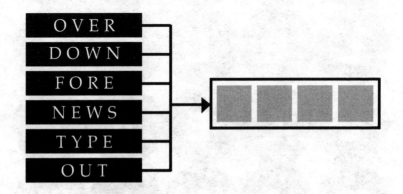

WORD PUZZLE 74

Which English word of four letters can be attached
to the back of the words shown in the diagram to
create six other words?

ANSWER 44

WORD PUZZLE 75

Select one letter from each of the segments.
When the correct letters have been found a word of
eight letters can be read clockwise.
What is the word?

ANSWER 85

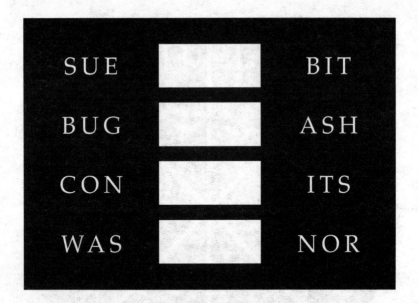

SUE		BIT
BUG		ASH
CON		ITS
WAS		NOR

WORD PUZZLE 76

Place two letters in the empty space which, when added to the end of the words to the left and to the beginning of the right, form other English words. When this is completed another word can be read down. What is the word?

ANSWER 33

T	A	W	S
E	V	E	I
L	S	N	O
D	H	W	C

WORD PUZZLE 77

Take the letters and arrange them correctly in the
column under which they appear. Once this has
been done a movie title will appear.
What is the movie?

ANSWER 75

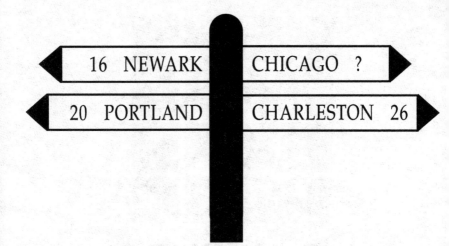

| 16 | NEWARK | CHICAGO | ? |
| 20 | PORTLAND | CHARLESTON | 26 |

WORD PUZZLE 78

This is a meaningless signpost but there is a twisted form of logic behind the figures. Discover the logic and find the distance to Chicago.
How far is it?

ANSWER 65

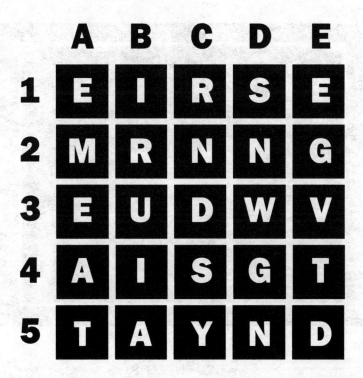

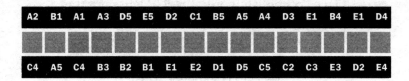

WORD PUZZLE 79

Select one of the two letters from the grid, in accordance with the reference shown, and place it in the word frame. When the correct letters have been chosen a sixteen-letter word can be read. What is the word?

ANSWER 23

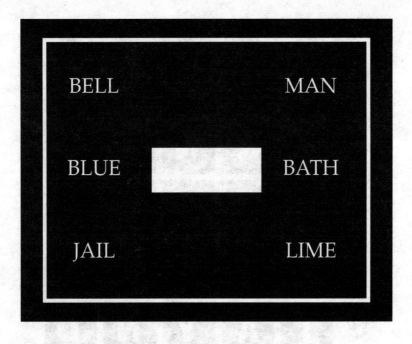

BELL   MAN

BLUE   BATH

JAIL   LIME

WORD PUZZLE 80

Place an English word of FOUR letters in the empty space. This word, when added to the end of the three words to the left and to the beginning of the three words to the right, will form six other words. What is the word?

ANSWER 13

WORD PUZZLE 81

Place one letter in the middle of this diagram. Four five-letter words can now be rearranged from each straight line of letters. What is the letter and what are the words?

ANSWER 54

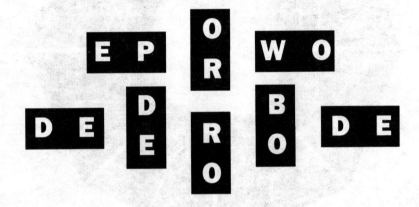

WORD PUZZLE 82

Arrange the tiles in this diagram so that they form
a square. When this is done correctly four words
can be read down and across. What are the words?

ANSWER 2

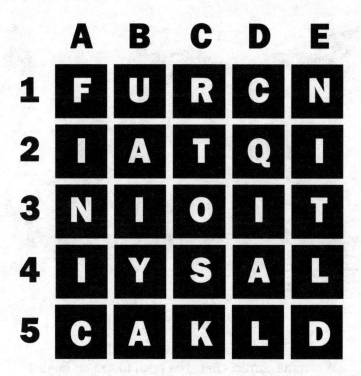

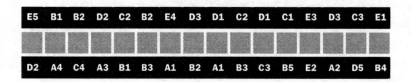

E5	B1	B2	D2	C2	B2	E4	D3	D1	C2	D1	C1	E3	D3	C3	E1
D2	A4	C4	A3	B1	B3	A1	B2	A1	B3	C3	B5	E2	A2	D5	B4

WORD PUZZLE 83

Select one of the two letters from the grid, in accordance with the reference shown, and place it in the word frame. When the correct letters have been chosen a sixteen-letter word can be read. What is the word?

ANSWER 95

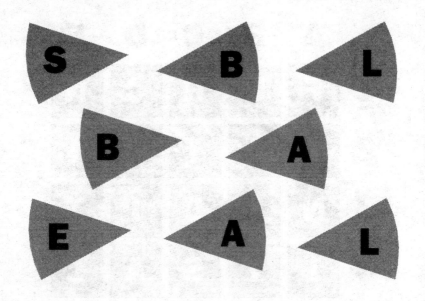

WORD PUZZLE 84

Make a circle out of these shapes.
When the correct circle has been found an English
word can be read clockwise. What is the word?

ANSWER 43

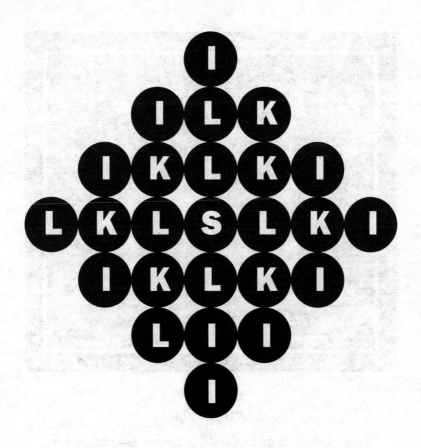

WORD PUZZLE 85

Move from circle to touching circle collecting the
letters of SILK. Always start at the S.
How many different ways are there to do this?

ANSWER 84

EPOCH	TULIP
SWINE	EXILE
OKAPI	ABBEY
DECOY	HIPPO
STEAM	BLOND

WORD PUZZLE 86

Five of the words in the diagram are associated for some reason. Find the words and then work out whether FLUTE belongs to the group.

ANSWER 32

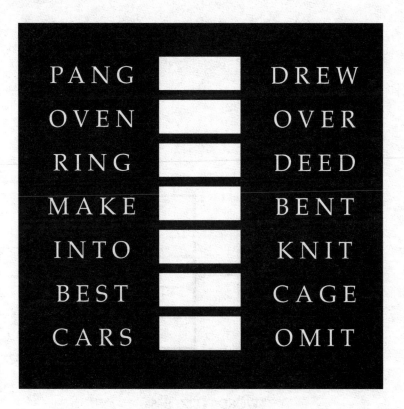

PANG		DREW
OVEN		OVER
RING		DEED
MAKE		BENT
INTO		KNIT
BEST		CAGE
CARS		OMIT

WORD PUZZLE 87

Change the first letter of each word to the left and
the right. Two other English words must be
formed. Place the letter used in the empty section.
When this has been completed for all the words
another English word can be read downwards.
What is the word?

ANSWER 74

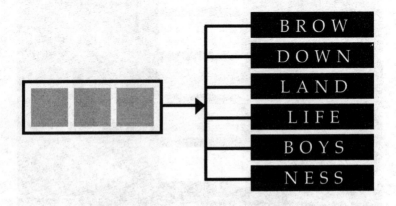

WORD PUZZLE 88

Which English word of three letters can be attached to the front of the words shown in the diagram to create six other words?

ANSWER 22

WORD PUZZLE 89

Complete the word ladder by changing one letter
of each word per step. The newly created word
must be found in the dictionary. What are the
words to turn LION to PUMA?

ANSWER 64

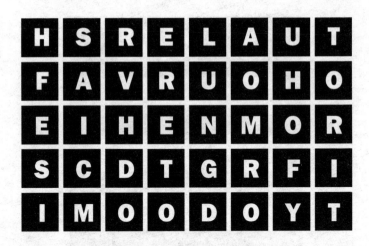

H	S	R	E	L	A	U	T
F	A	V	R	U	O	H	O
E	I	H	E	N	M	O	R
S	C	D	T	G	R	F	I
I	M	O	O	D	O	Y	T

WORD PUZZLE 90

A quotation has been written in this diagram.
Find the start letter and move from square to
touching square until you have found it. What is
the quotation and to whom is it attributed?

ANSWER 12

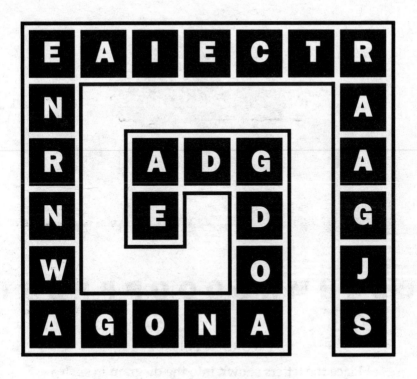

WORD PUZZLE 91

The names of three trees are to be found in the diagram. The letters of the names are in the order they normally appear. What are the trees?

ANSWER 53

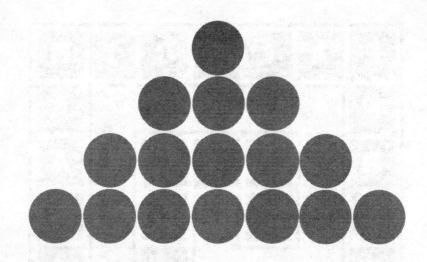

CDEHMNOOOOPPRSST

WORD PUZZLE 92

Place the letters shown into the diagram in such a way that three words can be read across and one down the middle. What are the words?

ANSWER 1

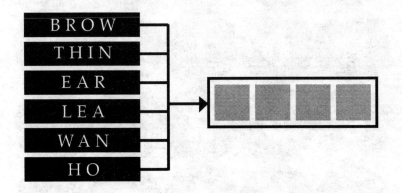

WORD PUZZLE 93

Which English word of four letters can be attached
to the back of the words shown in the diagram to
create six other words?

ANSWER 42

WORD PUZZLE 94

Start at the bottom letter A and move from circle to touching circle to the E at the top right. How many different ways are there of collecting the nine letters of ABORIGINE?

ANSWER 94

WORD PUZZLE 95

Select one letter from each of the segments.
When the correct letters have been found a word of
eight letters can be read clockwise.
What is the word?

ANSWER 83

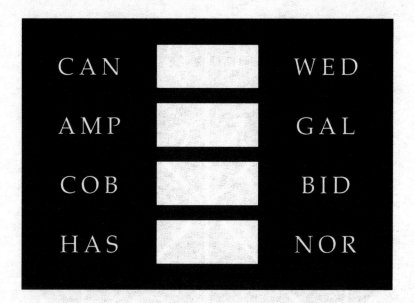

WORD PUZZLE 96

Place two letters in the empty space which, when added to the end of the words to the left and to the beginning of the right, form other English words. When this is completed another word can be read down. What is the word?

ANSWER 31

F	E	I	J
K	R	I	N
A	L	A	N
B	M	N	N

WORD PUZZLE 97

Take the letters and arrange them correctly in the column under which they appear. Once this has been done a famous person will appear.
Who is the person?

ANSWER 73

THE PROFESSIONAL WRESTLER WAS OF • • • • • • BUILD AND BORE A • • • • • • AGAINST HIS OPPONENT.

WORD PUZZLE 98

Two words using the same letters in their construction can be used to replace the dots in this sentence. The sentence will then make sense. Each dot is one letter. What are the words?

ANSWER 21

16   LONDON   YORK   11

23   LIVERPOOL   BIRMINGHAM   ?

WORD PUZZLE 99

The distances on this signpost are fictitious. They
bear a relationship to the letters in the names.
What should replace the question mark?

ANSWER 63

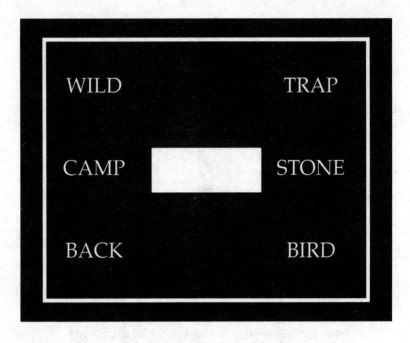

WORD PUZZLE 100

Place an English word of FOUR letters in the empty space. This word, when added to the end of the three words to the left and to the beginning of the three words to the right, will form six other words. What is the word?

ANSWER 11

WORD PUZZLE 101

Place one letter in the middle of this diagram. Four five-letter words can now be rearranged from each straight line of letters. What is the letter and what are the words?

ANSWER 52

WORD PUZZLE 102

Arrange the tiles in this diagram so that they form
a square. When this is done correctly five words
can be read downwards and across.
What are the words?

ANSWER 104

	A	B	C	D	E
1	S	U	A	T	N
2	O	L	T	T	N
3	R	A	N	U	I
4	T	L	C	Z	O
5	I	O	A	I	N

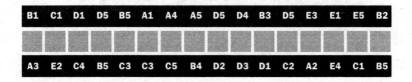

B1	C1	D1	D5	B5	A1	A4	A5	D5	D4	B3	D5	E3	E1	E5	B2
A3	E2	C4	B5	C3	C3	C5	B4	D2	D3	D1	C2	A2	E4	C1	B5

WORD PUZZLE 103

Select one of the two letters from the grid, in accordance with the reference shown, and place it in the word frame. When the correct letters have been chosen a sixteen-letter word can be read. What is the word?

ANSWER 93

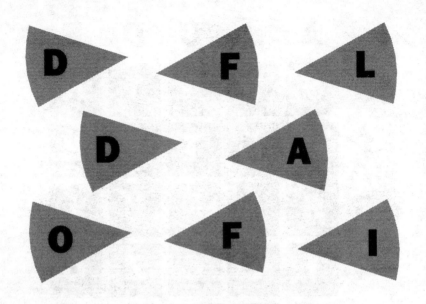

WORD PUZZLE 104

Make a circle out of these shapes.
When the correct circle has been found an English
word can be read clockwise. What is the word?

ANSWER 41

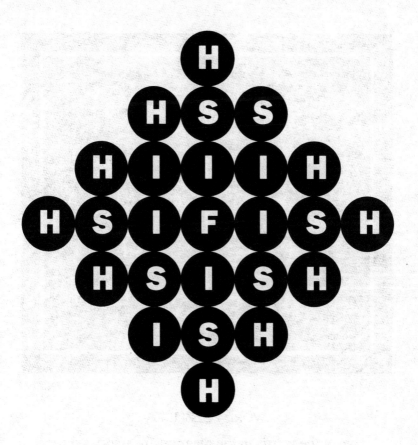

WORD PUZZLE 105

Move from circle to touching circle collecting the
letters of FISH. Always start at the F.
How many different ways are there to do this?

ANSWER 167

A S P I C	I M A G E
S T E E L	A N N O Y
L E A F Y	C O M M A
J E T T Y	A G E N T
B E A C H	C A D D Y

WORD PUZZLE 106

Five of the words in the diagram are associated for
some reason. Find the words and then work out
whether CHEER belongs to the group.

ANSWER 115

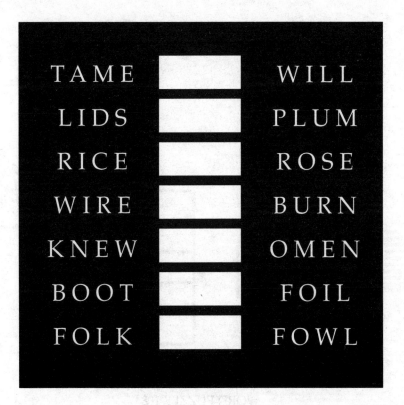

WORD PUZZLE 107

Change the first letter of each word to the left and
the right. Two other English words must be
formed. Place the letter used in the empty section.
When this has been completed for all the words
another English word can be read down.
What is the word?

ANSWER 134

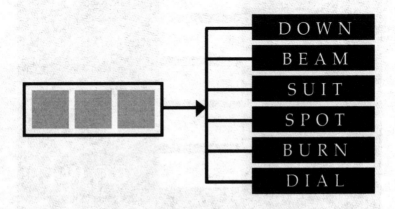

WORD PUZZLE 108

Which English word of three letters can be attached to the front of the words shown in the diagram to create six other words?

ANSWER 156

WORD PUZZLE 109

Complete the word ladder by changing one letter of each word per step. The newly created word must be found in the dictionary. What are the words to turn BLAZE to GLORY?

ANSWER 197

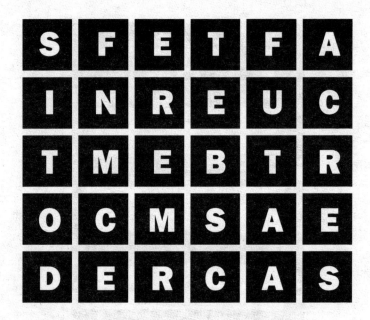

WORD PUZZLE 110

A quotation has been written in this diagram.
Find the start letter and move from square to
touching square until you have found it. What is
the quotation and to whom is it attributed?

ANSWER 145

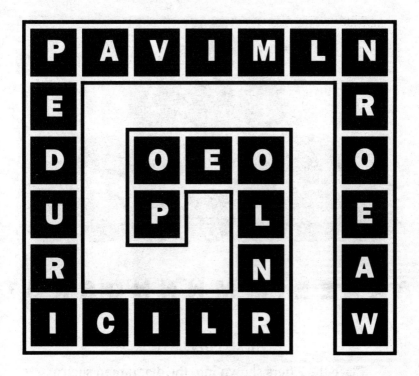

WORD PUZZLE 111

The names of three animals are to be found in the
diagram. The letters of the names are in the order
they normally appear. What are the animals?

ANSWER 166

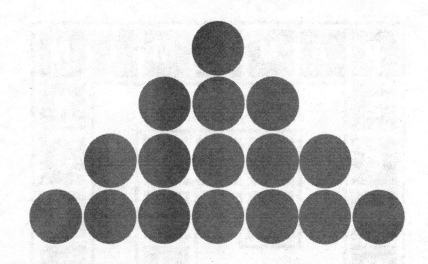

A A A E E I M M N N N O R R S T

WORD PUZZLE 112

Place the letters shown into the diagram in such a
way that three words can be read across and one
down the middle. What are the words?

ANSWER 114

WORD PUZZLE 113

Start at the bottom letter F and move from circle to
touching circle to the S at the top right. How many
different ways are there of collecting the nine
letters of FESTIVALS ?

ANSWER 125

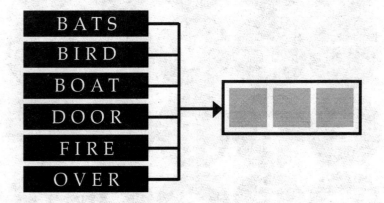

BATS
BIRD
BOAT
DOOR
FIRE
OVER

WORD PUZZLE 114

Which English word of three letters can be attached
to the back of the words shown in the diagram to
create six other words?

ANSWER 155

WORD PUZZLE 115

Select one letter from each of the segments.
When the correct letters have been found a word of
eight letters can be read clockwise.
What is the word?

ANSWER 196

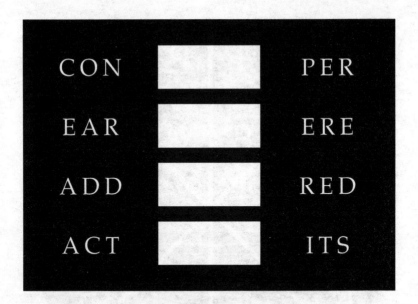

WORD PUZZLE 116

Place two letters in the empty space which, when
added to the end of the words to the left and to the
beginning of the right, form other English words.
When this is completed another word
can be read down. What is the word?

ANSWER 144

H	O	R	C
T	I	N	S
W	U	L	L
H	I	N	C

WORD PUZZLE 117

Take the letters and arrange them correctly in the column under which they appear. Once this has been done the name of a famous person will emerge. What is the name ?

ANSWER 186

WORD PUZZLE 118

Start at the bottom letter M and move from circle to
touching circle to the S at the top right. How many
different ways are there of collecting the nine
letters of MAGAZINES?

ANSWER 177

PIZZA	78
BURGER	71
STEAK	56
FRIES	?

On this list of stock the number of packets of each food are written . The numbers bear a relationship to the letters in the words. What should replace the question mark?

ANSWER 176

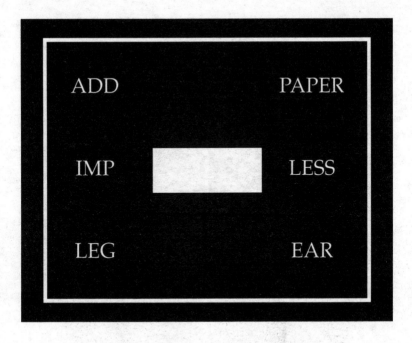

ADD

PAPER

IMP

LESS

LEG

EAR

WORD PUZZLE 120

Place an English word of THREE letters in the empty space. This word, when added to the end of the three words to the left and to the beginning of the three words to the right, will form six other words. What is the word?

ANSWER 124

WORD PUZZLE 121

Place one letter in the middle of this diagram. Four five-letter words can now be rearranged from each straight line of letters. What is the letter and what are the words?

ANSWER 165

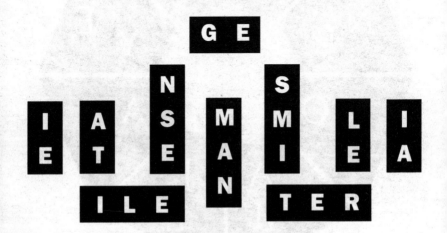

WORD PUZZLE 122

Arrange the tiles in this diagram so that they form
a square. When this is done correctly five words
can be read downwards and across.
What are the words?

ANSWER 113

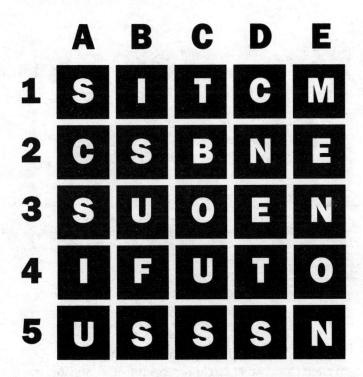

	A	B	C	D	E
1	S	I	T	C	M
2	C	S	B	N	E
3	S	U	O	E	N
4	I	F	U	T	O
5	U	S	S	S	N

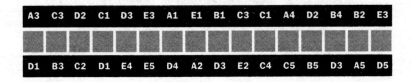

A3	C3	D2	C1	D3	E3	A1	E1	B1	C3	C1	A4	D2	B4	B2	E3
D1	B3	C2	D1	E4	E5	D4	A2	D3	E2	C4	C5	B5	D3	A5	D5

WORD PUZZLE 123

Select one of the two letters from the grid, in accordance with the reference shown, and place it in the word frame. When the correct letters have been chosen a sixteen-letter word can be read. What is the word?

ANSWER 206

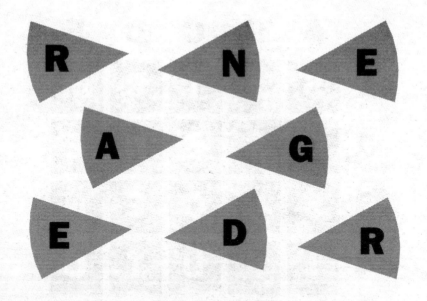

WORD PUZZLE 124

Make a circle out of these shapes.
When the correct circle has been found an English
word can be read clockwise. What is the word?

ANSWER 154

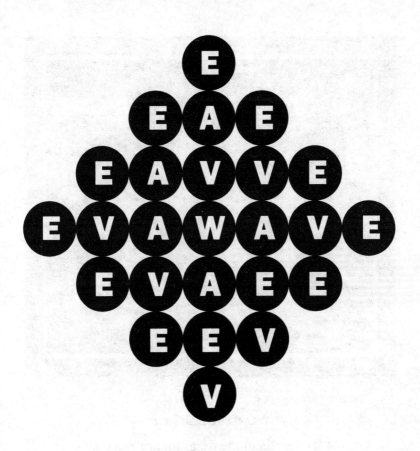

WORD PUZZLE 125

Move from circle to touching circle collecting the letters of WAVE. Always start at the W. How many different ways are there to do this?

ANSWER 195

BACON	BABES
GAMES	GIPSY
SUSHI	RESIN
PAPER	TALES
TRAIN	CAKES

WORD PUZZLE 126

Five of the words in the diagram are associated for some reason. Find the words and then work out whether CAFES belongs to the group.

ANSWER 143

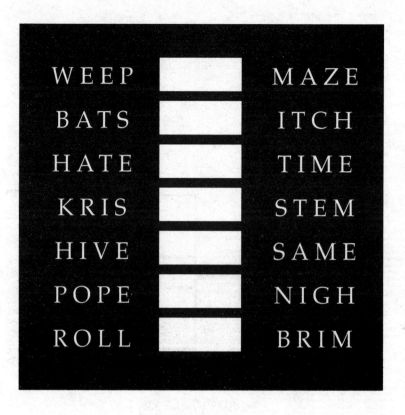

WORD PUZZLE 127

Change the first letter of each word to the left and the right. Two other English words must be formed. Place the letter used in the empty section. When this has been completed for all the words another English word can be read down.
What is the word?

ANSWER 185

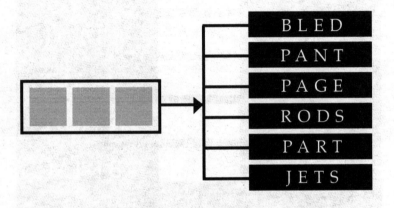

WORD PUZZLE 128

Which English word of three letters can be attached
to the front of the words shown in the diagram to
create six other words?

ANSWER 133

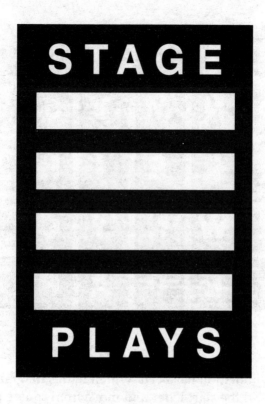

WORD PUZZLE 129

Complete the word ladder by changing one letter
of each word per step. The newly created word
must be found in the dictionary. What are the
words to turn STAGE to PLAYS?

ANSWER 175

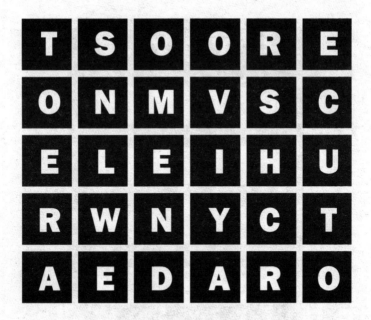

T	S	O	O	R	E
O	N	M	V	S	C
E	L	E	I	H	U
R	W	N	Y	C	T
A	E	D	A	R	O

WORD PUZZLE 130

A quotation has been written in this diagram.
Find the start letter and move from square to
touching square until you have found it. What is
the quotation and to whom is it attributed?

ANSWER 123

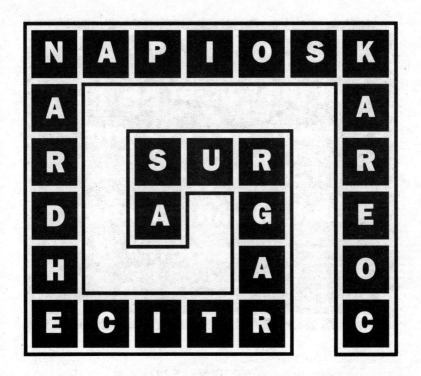

WORD PUZZLE 131

The names of three plants are to be found in the
diagram. The letters of the names are in the order
they normally appear. What are the plants?

ANSWER 164

IN THE FOREST AS THE

FRUIT • • • • • • THE

FURTIVE • • • • • •

LURKS IN ANTICIPATION

OF HIS VICTIM.

WORD PUZZLE 132

Two words using the same letters in their
construction can be used to replace the dots in this
sentence. The sentence will then make sense. Each
dot is one letter. What are the words?

ANSWER 112

S E O N

G H O R

G T W A

G E I N

WORD PUZZLE 133

Take the letters and arrange them correctly in the column under which they appear. Once this has been done the name of a famous person will emerge. What is the name?

ANSWER 184

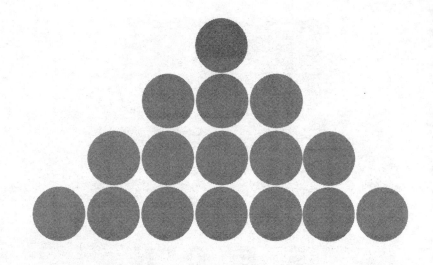

A A A B C D D E H I K L M N R Y

WORD PUZZLE 134

Place the letters shown into the diagram in such a
way that three words can be read across and one
down the middle. What are the words?

ANSWER 132

WORD PUZZLE 135

Select one letter from each of the segments.
When the correct letters have been found a word of
eight letters can be read clockwise.
What is the word?

ANSWER 194

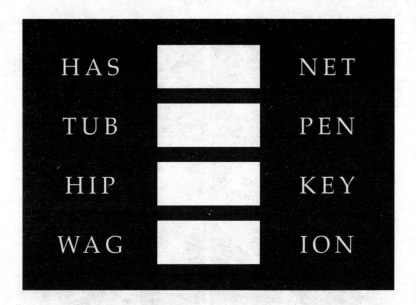

HAS		NET
TUB		PEN
HIP		KEY
WAG		ION

WORD PUZZLE 136

Place two letters in the empty space which, when added to the end of the words to the left and to the beginning of the right, form other English words. When this is completed another word can be read down. What is the word?

ANSWER 142

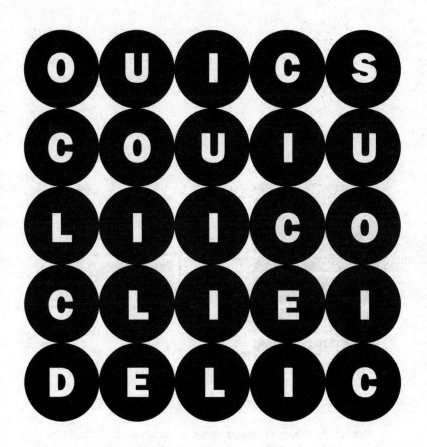

WORD PUZZLE 137

Start at the bottom letter D and move from circle to touching circle to the S at the top right. How many different ways are there of collecting the nine letters of DELICIOUS?

ANSWER 205

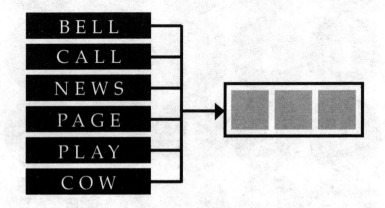

WORD PUZZLE 138

Which English word of three letters can be attached to the back of the words shown in the diagram to create six other words?

ANSWER 153

PIGS	71
SHEEP	78
BULLS	91
HORSES	?

WORD PUZZLE 139

On this list of farm stock the number of animals is written. The numbers bear a relationship to the letters in the words. What should replace the question mark?

ANSWER 174

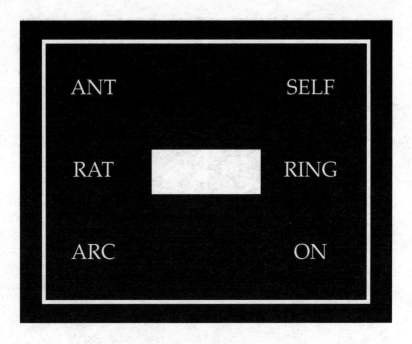

ANT   SELF

RAT   RING

ARC   ON

WORD PUZZLE 140

Place an English word of THREE letters in the empty space. This word, when added to the end of the three words to the left and to the beginning of the three words to the right, will form six other words. What is the word?

ANSWER 122

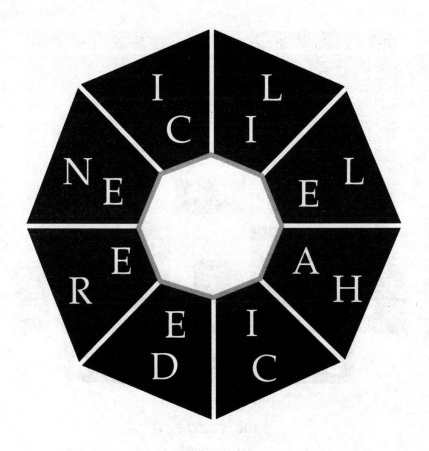

WORD PUZZLE 141

Place one letter in the middle of this diagram. Four
five-letter words can now be rearranged from each
straight line of letters. What is the letter and what
are the words?

ANSWER 163

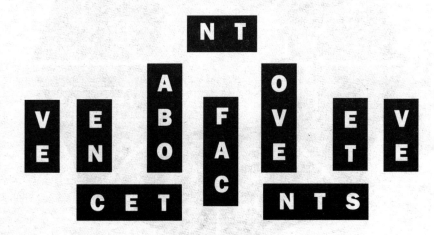

WORD PUZZLE 142

Arrange the tiles in this diagram so that they form
a square. When this is done correctly five words
can be read down and across. What are the words?

ANSWER 111

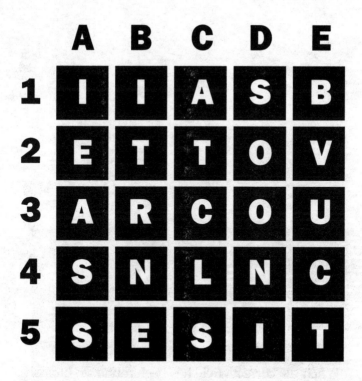

	A	B	C	D	E
1	I	I	A	S	B
2	E	T	T	O	V
3	A	R	C	O	U
4	S	N	L	N	C
5	S	E	S	I	T

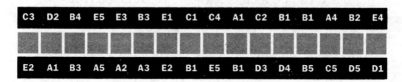

C3	D2	B4	E5	E3	B3	E1	C1	C4	A1	C2	B1	B1	A4	B2	E4

| E2 | A1 | B3 | A5 | A2 | A3 | E2 | B1 | E5 | B1 | D3 | D4 | B5 | C5 | D5 | D1 |

WORD PUZZLE 143

Select one of the two letters from the grid, in accordance with the reference shown, and place it in the word frame. When the correct letters have been chosen a sixteen-letter word can be read. What is the word?

ANSWER 204

WORD PUZZLE 144

Make a circle out of these shapes.
When the correct circle has been found an English
word can be read clockwise. What is the word?

ANSWER 152

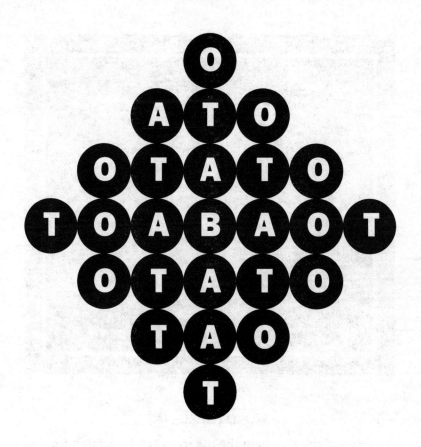

WORD PUZZLE 145

Move from circle to touching circle collecting the
letters of BOAT. Always start at the B.
How many different ways are there to do this?

ANSWER 193

STAGE	BREAD
TUTOR	DREAD
COMIC	YUCCA
LOYAL	ARENA
SAUNA	KIOSK

WORD PUZZLE 146

Five of the words in the diagram are associated for some reason. Find the words and then work out whether WIDOW belongs to the group.

ANSWER 141

THIN		RAGE
SKIN		FIRS
WIFE		BUMP
SOUR		TANK
DARK		MOST
CHIP		WEAR
WILY		BATH

WORD PUZZLE 147

Change the first letter of each word to the left and the right. Two other English words must be formed. Place the letter used in the empty section. When this has been completed for all the words another English word can be read down. What is the word?

ANSWER 183

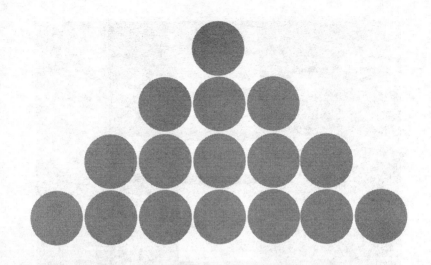

A A A B C E E E H M M M R T T Z

WORD PUZZLE 148

Place the letters shown into the diagram in such a
way that three words can be read across and one
down the middle. What are the words?

ANSWER 131

WORD PUZZLE 149

Complete the word ladder by changing one letter
of each word per step. The newly created word
must be found in the dictionary. What are the
words to turn DROP to FALL?

ANSWER 173

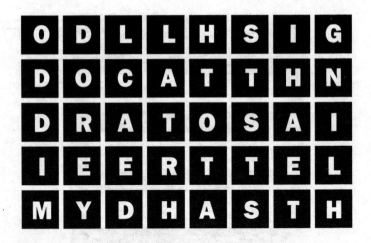

O	D	L	L	H	S	I	G
D	O	C	A	T	T	H	N
D	R	A	T	O	S	A	I
I	E	E	R	T	T	E	L
M	Y	D	H	A	S	T	H

WORD PUZZLE 150

A quotation has been written in this diagram.
Find the start letter and move from square to
touching square until you have found it. What is
the quotation and to whom is it attributed?

ANSWER 121

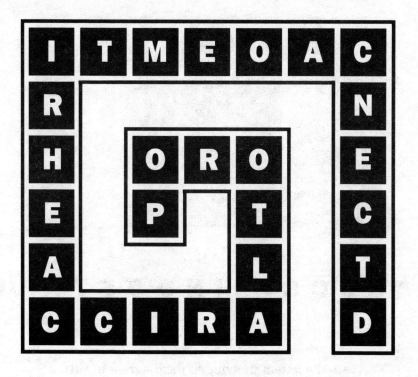

WORD PUZZLE 151

The names of three professions are to be found in
the diagram. The letters of the names are in the
order they normally appear.
What are the professions?

ANSWER 162

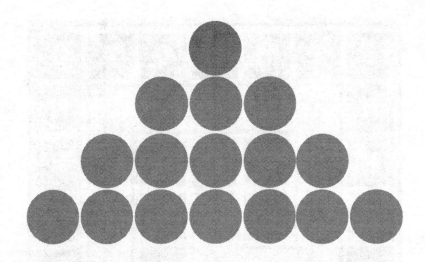

A B C C H I I N O O S T T T U

WORD PUZZLE 152

Place the letters shown into the diagram in such a
way that three words can be read across and one
down the middle. What are the words?

ANSWER 110

THE VALUABLE
SCIENTIFIC EQUIPMENT
WAS CAREFULLY • • • • • •
AND CHECKED BEFORE
BEING • • • • • • TO
THE OTHER SIDE OF
THE BUILDING.

WORD PUZZLE 153

Two words using the same letters in their construction can be used to replace the dots in this sentence. The sentence will then make sense. Each dot is one letter. What are the words?

ANSWER 203

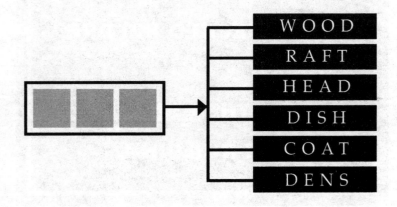

WORD PUZZLE 154

Which English word of three letters can be attached to the front of the words shown in the diagram to create six other words?

ANSWER 151

WORD PUZZLE 155

Select one letter from each of the segments.
When the correct letters have been found a word of
eight letters can be read clockwise.
What is the word?

ANSWER 192

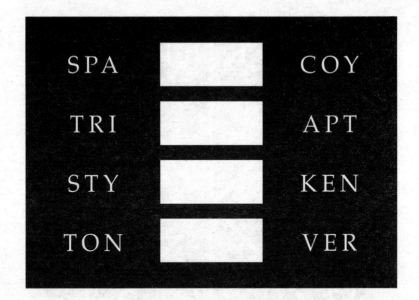

WORD PUZZLE 156

Place two letters in the empty space which, when
added to the end of the words to the left and to the
beginning of the right, form other English words.
When this is completed another word
can be read down. What is the word?

ANSWER 140

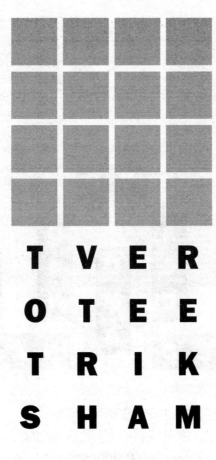

T	V	E	R
O	T	E	E
T	R	I	K
S	H	A	M

WORD PUZZLE 157

Take the letters and arrange them correctly in the column under which they appear. Once this has been done the name of a film will emerge.
What is it?

ANSWER 182

WORD PUZZLE 158

Arrange the tiles in this diagram so that they form
a square. When this is done correctly five words
can be read down and across. What are the words?

ANSWER 130

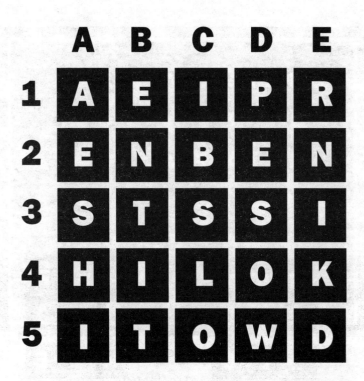

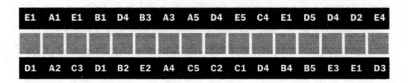

WORD PUZZLE 159

Select one of the two letters from the grid, in accordance with the reference shown, and place it in the word frame. When the correct letters have been chosen a sixteen-letter word can be read. What is the word?

ANSWER 172

THE LANGUAGE USED
BY THE • • • • • • AT
THE BASEBALL GAME
WAS SO • • • • • •
IT WAS SCARCELY
UNDERSTANDABLE.

WORD PUZZLE 160

Two words using the same letters in their
construction can be used to replace the dots in this
sentence. The sentence will then make sense. Each
dot is one letter. What are the words?

ANSWER 120

WORD PUZZLE 161

Place one letter in the middle of this diagram. Four five-letter words can now be rearranged from each straight line of letters. What is the letter and what are the words?

ANSWER 161

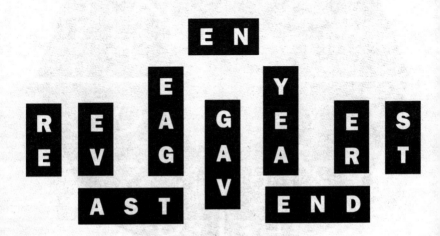

WORD PUZZLE 162

Arrange the tiles in this diagram so that they form
a square. When this is done correctly five words
can be read downwards and across.
What are the words?

ANSWER 109

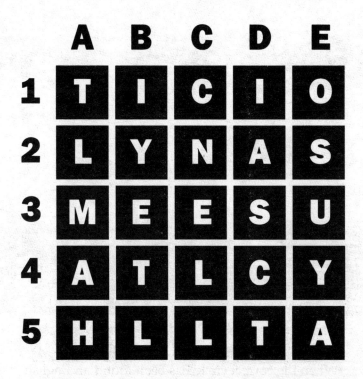

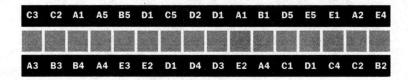

| C3 | C2 | A1 | A5 | B5 | D1 | C5 | D2 | D1 | A1 | B1 | D5 | E5 | E1 | A2 | E4 |

| A3 | B3 | B4 | A4 | E3 | E2 | D1 | D4 | D3 | E2 | A4 | C1 | D1 | C4 | C2 | B2 |

WORD PUZZLE 163

Select one of the two letters from the grid, in
accordance with the reference shown, and place it
in the word frame. When the correct letters have
been chosen a sixteen-letter word can be read.
What is the word?

ANSWER 202

WORD PUZZLE 164

Make a circle out of these shapes.
When the correct circle has been found an English
word can be read clockwise. What is the word?

ANSWER 150

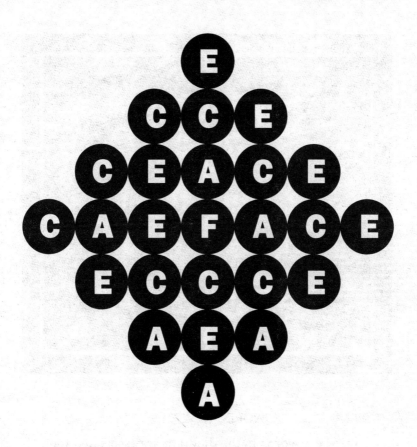

WORD PUZZLE 165

Move from circle to touching circle collecting the
letters of FACE. Always start at the F.
How many different ways are there to do this?

ANSWER 191

HYMNS	LIGHT
SHRUB	FILMS
PIZZA	QUEEN
ANKLE	FLAME
PASTA	INDEX

WORD PUZZLE 166

Six of the words in the diagram are associated for some reason. Find the words and then work out whether GLOBE belongs to the group.

ANSWER 139

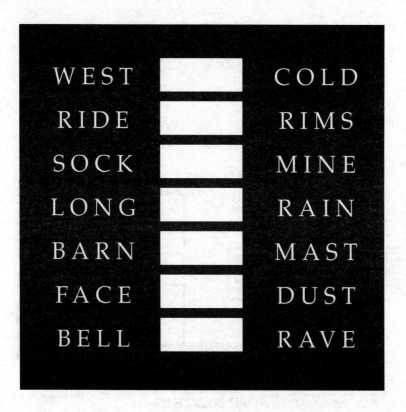

WEST		COLD
RIDE		RIMS
SOCK		MINE
LONG		RAIN
BARN		MAST
FACE		DUST
BELL		RAVE

WORD PUZZLE 167

Change the first letter of each word to the left and the right. Two other English words must be formed. Place the letter used in the empty section. When this has been completed for all the words another English word can be read down.
What is the word?

ANSWER 181

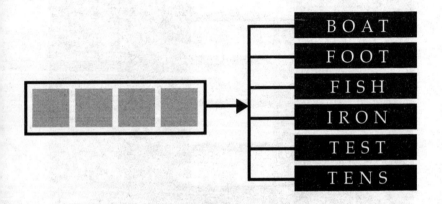

WORD PUZZLE 168

Which English word of four letters can be attached to the front of the words shown in the diagram to create six other words?

ANSWER 129

WORD PUZZLE 169

Complete the word ladder by changing one letter
of each word per step. The newly created word
must be found in the dictionary. What are the
words to turn PORT to SHIP?

ANSWER 171

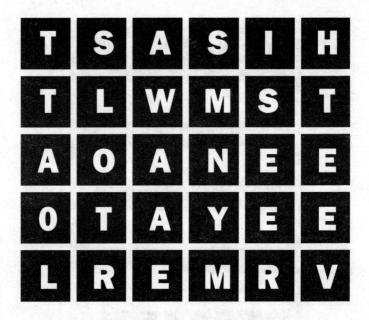

T	S	A	S	I	H
T	L	W	M	S	T
A	O	A	N	E	E
O	T	A	Y	E	E
L	R	E	M	R	V

WORD PUZZLE 170

A quotation has been written in this diagram.
Find the start letter and move from square to
touching square until you have found it. What is
the quotation and to whom is it attributed?

ANSWER 119

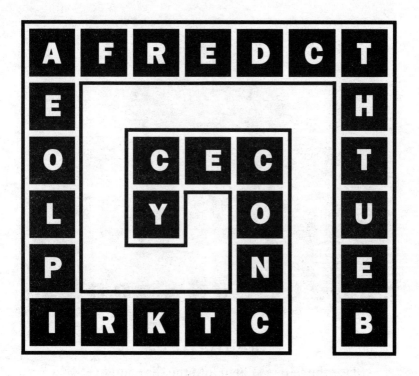

WORD PUZZLE 171

The names of three insects are to be found in the diagram. The letters of the names are in the order they normally appear. What are the insects?

ANSWER 160

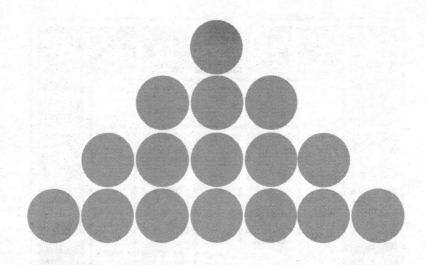

AAABCCEHNNOORSST

WORD PUZZLE 172

Place the letters shown into the diagram in such a way that three words can be read across and one down the middle. What are the words?

ANSWER 108

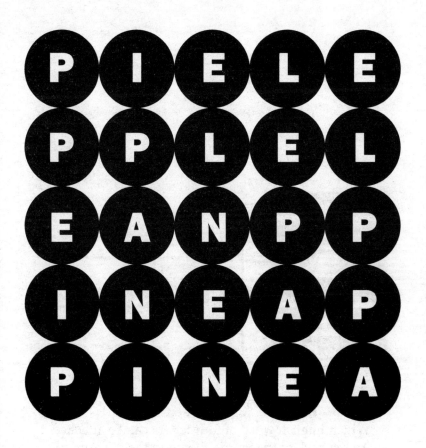

WORD PUZZLE 173

Start at the bottom letter P and move from circle to touching circle to the E at the top right. How many different ways are there of collecting the nine letters of PINEAPPLE?

ANSWER 201

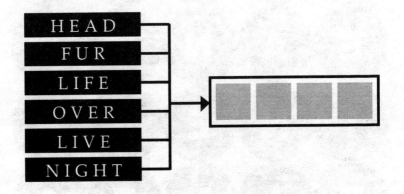

WORD PUZZLE 174

Which English word of four letters can be attached
to the back of the words shown in the diagram to
create six other words?

ANSWER 149

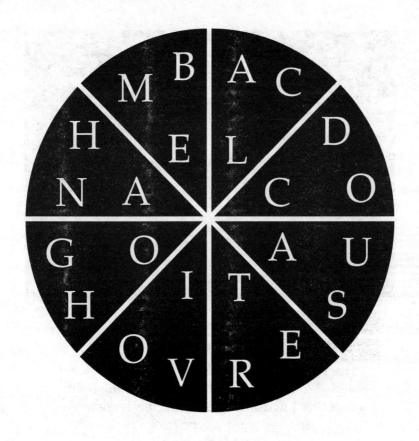

WORD PUZZLE 175

Select one letter from each of the segments.
When the correct letters have been found a word of
eight letters can be read clockwise.
What is the word?

ANSWER 190

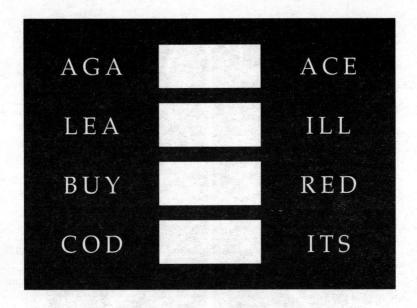

AGA		ACE
LEA		ILL
BUY		RED
COD		ITS

WORD PUZZLE 176

Place two letters in the empty space which, when added to the words to the left and to the right, form other English words. When this is completed another word can be read down.
What is the word?

ANSWER 138

W T F L

E I A I

T O C S

A O E T

WORD PUZZLE 177

Take the letters and arrange them correctly in the column under which they appear. Once this has been done the name of a novel and a movie will emerge. What is it?

ANSWER 180

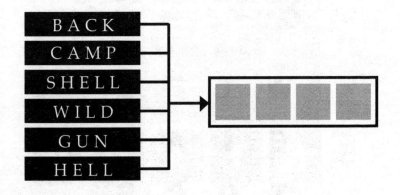

WORD PUZZLE 178

Which English word of four letters can be attached
to the back of the words shown in the diagram to
create six other words?

ANSWER 128

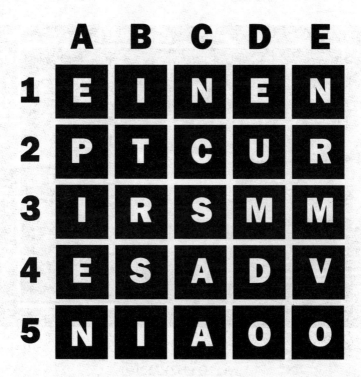

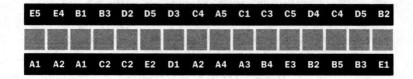

| E5 | E4 | B1 | B3 | D2 | D5 | D3 | C4 | A5 | C1 | C3 | C5 | D4 | C4 | D5 | B2 |
| A1 | A2 | A1 | C2 | C2 | E2 | D1 | A2 | A4 | A3 | B4 | E3 | B2 | B5 | B3 | E1 |

WORD PUZZLE 179

Select one of the two letters from the grid, in accordance with the reference shown, and place it in the word frame. When the correct letters have been chosen a sixteen-letter word can be read. What is the word?

ANSWER 170

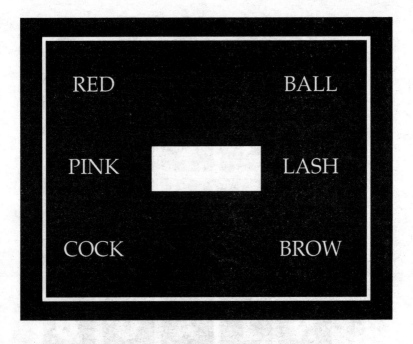

RED		BALL
PINK		LASH
COCK		BROW

WORD PUZZLE 180

Place an English word of THREE letters in the empty space. This word, when added to the end of the three words to the left and to the beginning of the three words to the right, will form six other words. What is the word?

ANSWER 118

WORD PUZZLE 181

Place one letter in the middle of this diagram.
Four five-letter words can now be rearranged from
each straight line of letters. What is the letter and what
are the words?

ANSWER 159

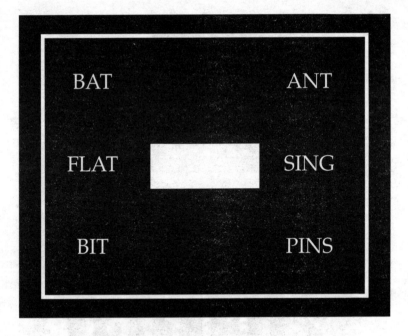

BAT

ANT

FLAT

SING

BIT

PINS

WORD PUZZLE 182

Place an English word of THREE letters in the empty space. This word, when added to the end of the three words to the left and to the beginning of the three words to the right, will form six other words. What is the word?

ANSWER 107

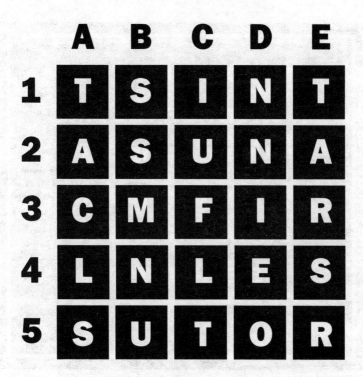

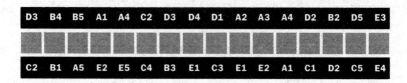

WORD PUZZLE 183

Select one of the two letters from the grid, in accordance with the reference shown, and place it in the word frame. When the correct letters have been chosen a sixteen-letter word can be read. What is the word?

ANSWER 200

THE CAVE MAN SAT

IN FRONT OF THE FIRE,

HOLDING A PIECE OF

• • • • • ON HIS KNEE,

ON WHICH WAS TO

BE FOUND SOME

• • • • • FOOD.

WORD PUZZLE 184

Two words using the same letters in their
construction can be used to replace the dots in this
sentence. The sentence will then make sense. Each
dot is one letter. What are the words?

ANSWER 148

WORD PUZZLE 185

Move from circle to touching circle collecting the
letters of DIET. Always start at the D.
How many different ways are there to do this?

ANSWER 189

SIREN	SWORD
DENIM	VASES
WIDOW	FOCUS
TIARA	LOTUS
MELON	RUPEE

WORD PUZZLE 186

Five of the words in the diagram are associated for some reason. Find the words and then work out whether VISOR belongs to the group.

ANSWER 137

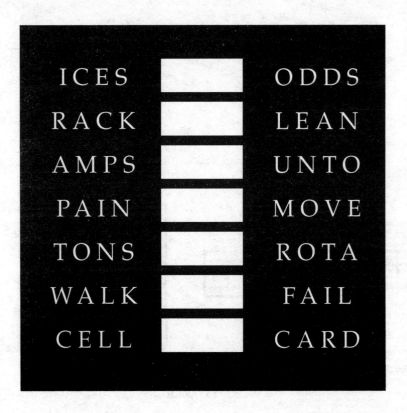

ICES		ODDS
RACK		LEAN
AMPS		UNTO
PAIN		MOVE
TONS		ROTA
WALK		FAIL
CELL		CARD

WORD PUZZLE 187

Change the first letter of each word to the left and
the right. Two other English words must be
formed. Place the letter used in the empty section.
When this has been completed for all the words
another English word can be read down.
What is the word?

ANSWER 179

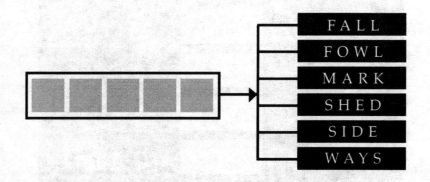

WORD PUZZLE 188

Which English word of five letters can be attached
to the front of the words shown in the diagram to
create six other words?

ANSWER 127

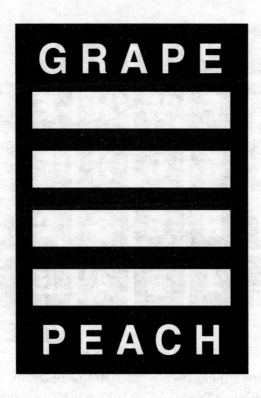

GRAPE

PEACH

WORD PUZZLE 189

Complete the word ladder by changing one letter
of each word per step. The newly created word
must be found in the dictionary. What are the
words to turn GRAPE to PEACH?

ANSWER 169

D	N	O	T	S	K
E	F	W	H	E	A
R	R	O	H	E	M
G	R	E	S	C	E
T	A	B	A	E	N

WORD PUZZLE 190

A proverb has been written in this diagram. Find the start letter and move from square to touching square until you have found it. What is it?

ANSWER 117

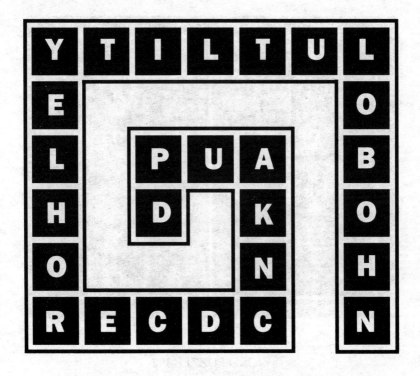

WORD PUZZLE 191
The names of three flowers are to be found in the diagram. The letters of the names are in the order they normally appear. What are the flowers?

ANSWER 158

APRIL	56
MAY	39
JUNE	?
JULY	68

WORD PUZZLE 192

The diagram shows the sunshine hours in England for four months. The numbers bear a relationship to the letters in the words. What should replace the question mark?

ANSWER 106

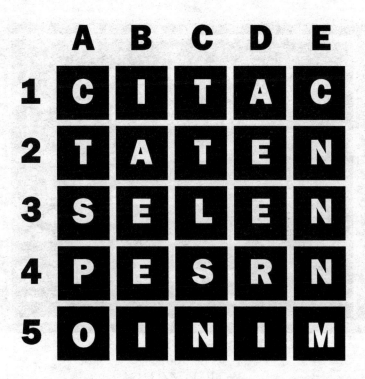

	A	B	C	D	E
1	C	I	T	A	C
2	T	A	T	E	N
3	S	E	L	E	N
4	P	E	S	R	N
5	O	I	N	I	M

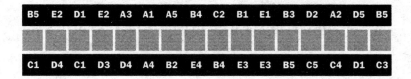

B5	E2	D1	E2	A3	A1	A5	B4	C2	B1	E1	B3	D2	A2	D5	B5
C1	D4	C1	D3	D4	A4	B2	E4	B4	E3	E3	B5	C5	C4	D1	C3

WORD PUZZLE 193

Select one of the two letters from the grid, in accordance with the reference shown, and place it in the word frame. When the correct letters have been chosen a sixteen-letter word can be read. What is the word?

ANSWER 199

THE WEIGHT LIFTER, ALTHOUGH VERY • • • • • •, FAILED IN HIS ATTEMPT BECAUSE OF HIS • • • • • • APPROACH.

WORD PUZZLE 194

Two words using the same letters in their construction can be used to replace the dots in this sentence. The sentence will then make sense. Each dot is one letter. What are the words?

ANSWER 147

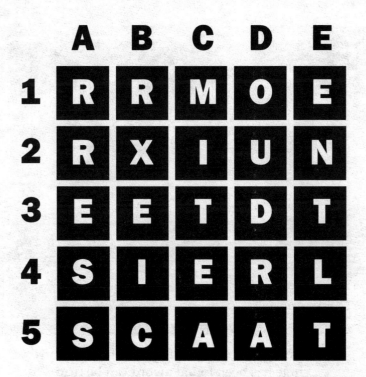

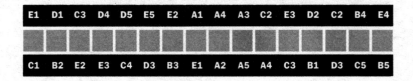

WORD PUZZLE 195

Select one of the two letters from the grid, in accordance with the reference shown, and place it in the word frame. When the correct letters have been chosen a sixteen-letter word can be read. What is the word?

ANSWER 188

WORD PUZZLE 196

Make a circle out of these shapes. When the correct circle has been found a word can be read clockwise. What is the word?

ANSWER 136

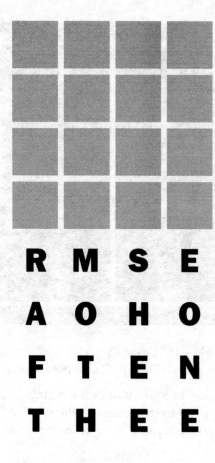

R M S E
A O H O
F T E N
T H E E

WORD PUZZLE 197

Take the letters and arrange them correctly in the
column under which they appear. Once this has
been done the name of a movie will emerge.
What is it?

ANSWER 178

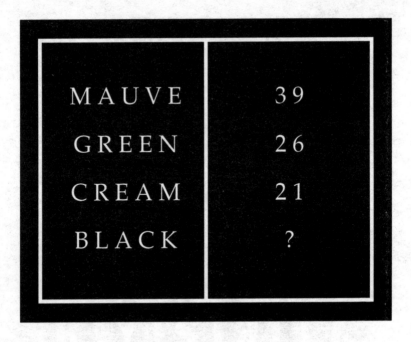

MAUVE	39
GREEN	26
CREAM	21
BLACK	?

WORD PUZZLE 198

On this list of four colours the numbers bear a relationship to the letters in the words. What should replace the question mark?

ANSWER 126

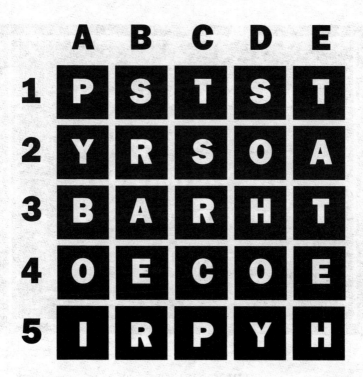

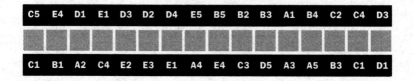

WORD PUZZLE 199

Select one of the two letters from the grid, in accordance with the reference shown, and place it in the word frame. When the correct letters have been chosen a sixteen-letter word can be read. What is the word?

ANSWER 168

THE PYTHON WOUND • • • • • • AROUND THE VICTIM AS IT ATTEMPTED TO • • • • • • IT TO DEATH.

WORD PUZZLE 200

Two words using the same letters in their construction can be used to replace the dots in this sentence. The sentence will then make sense. Each dot is one letter. What are the words?

ANSWER 116

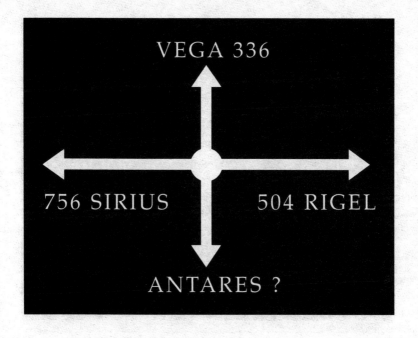

VEGA 336

756 SIRIUS

504 RIGEL

ANTARES ?

WORD PUZZLE 201

The diagram shows the light years to various stars. The numbers bear a relationship to the letters in the words. What should replace the question mark?

ANSWER 157

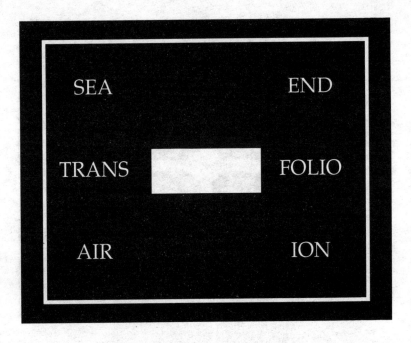

SEA   END

TRANS   FOLIO

AIR   ION

WORD PUZZLE 202

Place an English word of FOUR letters in the empty space. This word, when added to the end of the three words to the left and to the beginning of the three words to the right, will form six other words. What is the word?

ANSWER 105

WORD PUZZLE 203

Select one letter from each of the segments.
When the correct letters have been found a word of
eight letters can be read clockwise.
What is the word?

ANSWER 198

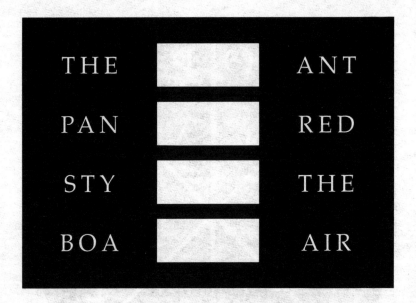

THE		ANT
PAN		RED
STY		THE
BOA		AIR

WORD PUZZLE 204

Place two letters in the empty space which, when added to the words to the left and to the right, form other English words. When this is completed another word can be read down.
What is the word?

ANSWER 146

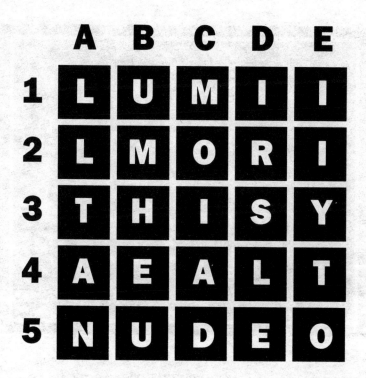

	A	B	C	D	E
1	L	U	M	I	I
2	L	M	O	R	I
3	T	H	I	S	Y
4	A	E	A	L	T
5	N	U	D	E	O

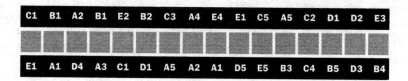

C1	B1	A2	B1	E2	B2	C3	A4	E4	E1	C5	A5	C2	D1	D2	E3
E1	A1	D4	A3	C1	D1	A5	A2	A1	D5	E5	B3	C4	B5	D3	B4

WORD PUZZLE 205

Select one of the two letters from the grid, in
accordance with the reference shown, and place it
in the word frame. When the correct letters have
been chosen a sixteen-letter word can be read.
What is the word?

ANSWER 187

IN THE FOREST FIRE THE UNDERGROWTH • • • • • • • IN THE FLAMES AS THE TREE • • • • • • •.

WORD PUZZLE 206

Two words using the same letters in their construction can be used to replace the dots in this sentence. The sentence will then make sense. Each dot is one letter. What are the words?

ANSWER 135

Answers

1. Ohm, Stoop, Respond, and Chop.

2. Word, Oboe, Rode, and Deep.

3. Mow, Jewel, Blanket, and Down.

4. Back, Aeon, Cove, and Knew.

5. Ivy, Geese, Embrace, and Over.

6. Yard, Afar, Race, and Drew.

7. Fir, First, Firearm, and Fire.

8. Stop, Tame, Omen, and Pent.

9. Lid, Valid, Quality, and Will.

10. Tide, Idea, Deer, and Ears

11. Fire.

12. Rulers have no authority from God to do mischief. Jonathan Mayhew.

13. Bird.

14. The first casualty when war comes is truth. Hiram Johnson.

15. Well.

16. All animals are equal but some animals are more equal than others. George Orwell.

17. Like.

18. If you can't stand the heat keep out of the kitchen. President Harry Truman.

19. Den.

20. When you have to kill a man it costs nothing to be polite. Winston Churchill.

21. Rugged and Grudge.

22. Low.

23. Misunderstanding.

24. Buck.

25. 192. Each vowel is worth 6 and each consonant 8. The vowels are added together, as are the consonants. The totals are then multiplied.

26. Foot.

27. Brides and Debris.

28. Hand.

29. 21 ways.

30. Moon.

31. Tolerate.

32. Flute does not belong to the group. The five associated words are Decoy, Steam, Tulip, Abbey, and Hippo. The first two letters of each word are in alphabetical order.

33. Delegate.

34.   12 ways.

35.   Imposter.

36.   8 ways.

37.   Operator.

38.   9 ways.

39.   Reunites.

40.   Shell does not belong to the group. The linked words are Beast, Decor, Heron, Human, Pilaf, and Round. The first and last letter position in the alphabet totals 22.

41.   Daffodil.

42.   Nest.

43.   Baseball.

44.   Cast.

45.   Woodbine.

46.   Band.

47.   Taxpayer.

48.   Step.

49.   Aardvark.

50.   House.

51.   Kindness.

52.   B. To give Elbow, Orbit, Habit, and Noble.

53.   Satinwood, Jacaranda, and Greengage.

54.   A. To give Koala, Peace, Shade, and Whale.

55.   Cannelloni, Macaroni, and Spaghetti.

56.   J. To give Enjoy, Major, Rajah, and Dojos.

57. Champagne, Chocolate, and Orangeade.

58. H. To give Abhor, Ethic, Ochre, and Usher.

59. Harmonium, Accordion, Piano, and Tuba.

60. P. To give Capon, Hippo, Imply, and Paper.

61. Argentina, Australia, and Indonesia.

62. G. To give Angel, Anger, Cigar, and Logic.

63. 27. Each vowel is worth 2 and each consonant 3. The totals of the vowels and consonants are added.

64. Loon, Loop, Poop, Pomp, Pump.

65. 20. Each vowel is worth 4 and each consonant 2. The totals of the vowels and consonants are added.

66. Pong, Pang, Rang, Rant, Cant.

67. Summer Vacations.

68. Raver, Raves, Paves, Pares, Bares, Barks.

69. 57. Each letter is given its positional value in the alphabet and these are added together.

70. Shop, Shoe, Sloe, Floe, Flee, Free.

71. 108. Each vowel in the name is worth 10 and each consonant is worth 22. These are all added together to give the distance.

72. Sleds, Slews, Slows, Glows, Grows, Gross.

73. Benjamin Franklin.

74. Gesture.

75. Dances with Wolves.

76. Rainbow.

77. The Spy Who Loved Me.

78. Emerald.

79. Oscar Hammerstein.

80. Magenta.

81. Mary, Queen of Scots.

82. Crimson.

83. Nineteen.

84. 17 ways.

85. Journals.

86. Style belongs to the group. The linked words are

Abyss, Buyer, Coypu, Idyll, and Mayor. All other words have Y as the third letter.

87. Historic.

88. Syrup does not belong to the group. The linked words are Cedar, Hedge, Medal, Sedan, and Wedge. All the words contain ED.

89. February.

90. Plant belongs to the group. The linked words are Burnt, Count, Event, Flint, and Giant. All the words end in NT.

91. Caffeine.

92. 5 ways

93. Unconstitutional.

94. 26 ways.

95. Disqualification.

96. 9 ways.

97. Characterization.

98. 22 ways.

99. Air-conditioning.

100. 14 ways.

101. Thanksgiving day.

102. 25 ways.

103. Acknowledgements.

104. Tango, Alien, Nines, Geese, and Onset.

105. Port.

106. 50. The alphabetical values of the letters are added together.

107. Ten.

108. Sat, Bacon, Anchors, and Each.

109. Yeast, Eager, Agave, Seven, and Trend.

110. Cot, Attic, Cushion, and Both.

111. Facet, Above, Coven, Event, and Tents.

112. Ripens and Sniper.

113. Smile, Mania, Inset, Liege, and Eater.

114. Arm, Enter, Mansion, and Arts.

115. Cheer does belong to the group. The associated words are Jetty, Comma, Annoy, Caddy, and Steel. Each have double letters.

116. Itself and Stifle.

117. Absence makes the heart grow fonder.

118. Eye.

119. Every man meets his Waterloo at last. Wendell Phillips.

120. Umpire and Impure.

121. Die my dear doctor thats the last thing I shall do. Lord Palmerston

122. Her.

123. One more such victory and we are lost. Pyrrhus.

124. End.

125. 6 ways.

126. 14. The alphabetical values of the first, third and fifth letters are added together.

127. Water.

128. Fire.

129. Flat.

130. Dance, Acorn, Nomad, Crave, and Ended.

131. Met, Amaze, Chamber, and Team.

132. Had, Blink, Academy, and Raid.

133. Ram.

134. Fantasy.

135. Writhes and Withers.

136. Macaroni.

137. Visor belongs to the group. The associated words are Vases, Denim, Widow, Focus, and Lotus. In each word the vowels appear in alphabetical order.

138. Pestered.

139. Globe does not belong to the group. The associated words are Hymns, Light, Ankle, Films, Index, and Pasta. Each word contains two letters next to each other which appear consecutively in the alphabet.

140. Deadline.

141. Widow belongs to the group. The associated words are Dread, Kiosk, Loyal, Arena, and Comic. Each word begins and ends with the same letter.

142. Teaspoon.

143. Cafes belongs to the group. The associated words are Babes, Games, Cakes, Paper, and Tales. Each have A

and E as their second and fourth letter.

144. Gathered.

145. Comment is free but facts are sacred. C.P. Scott.

146. Medalist.

147. Muscly and Clumsy.

148. Slate and Stale.

149. Long.

150. Jealousy.

151. Red.

152. Suitcase.

153. Boy.

154. Gardener.

155. Man.

156. Sun.

157. 1008. Each consonant is worth 7 and each vowel 12. The consonant total is multiplied by the vowel total.

158. Hollyhock, Buttercup, and Dandelion.

159. S. To give Basic, Eased, Haste (or Heats), and Music.

160. Butterfly, Centipede, and Cockroach.

161. E. To give Agent, Bleak, Enemy, and Query.

162. Decorator, Policeman, and Architect.

163. V. To give Civic, Devil, Haven, and Lever.

164. Coriander, Asparagus, and Artichoke.

165. K. To give Joked, Maker, Taken, and Yokel.

166. Wolverine , Armadillo, and Porcupine.

167. 16 ways.

168. Psychotherapists.

169. Grace, Glace, Place, Peace.

170. Overcompensation.

171. Sort, Soot, Shot, Shop.

172. Responsibilities.

173. Prop, Poop, Pool, Poll, Pall.

174. 114. A is given the value 6, B is given 7 and so forth. The letter values in each word are added together.

175. Stare, Stars, Stays, Slays.

176. 57. The first and last letters are given the value of their position in the alphabet. These are then added together.

177. 5 ways.

178. The Name of the Rose.

179. Ability.

180. A Tale of Two Cities.

181. Badgers.

182. Star Trek the Movie.

183. Calypso.

184. George Washington.

185. Delight.

186. Winston Churchill.

187. Multimillionaire.

188. Extraterrestrial.

189. 11 ways.

190. Macaroon

191. 18 ways.

192. Ultimate.

193. 16 ways.

194. Horsefly.

195. 21 ways.

196. Puzzlers.

197. Glaze, Glare, Glary.

198. Radiance.

199. Intercontinental.

200. Instrumentalists

201. 10 ways.

202. Enthusiastically.

203. Crated and Carted.

204. Conservationists.

205. 8 ways.

206. Subconsciousness.